CRITICAL ACCLAIM for
THE ANXIOUS TRAVELER

"Essential reading." – Marianne McClary, *The Good Day Sacramento Show*

"An impressive achievement." – Josh Noel, *The Chicago Tribune*

"An amazing message... a must-read for today." – Kathryn Zox, *VoiceAmerica*

"If you find yourself worrying about that next trip, I'd suggest finding a copy of *The Anxious Traveler* and reading it." – Milt Gross, *The Republican Journal*

"Incredibly insightful and informative." – *Magic City Morning Star*

"Brave and fascinating." – Sam McManis, *The Sacramento Bee*

THE ANXIOUS TRAVELER:
How to Overcome Your Fear to Travel the World

Rita Anya Nara

Antareura
Media

FIRST EDITION, JUNE 2013
SAN FRANCISCO, CALIFORNIA

The anxious traveler: how to overcome your fear to travel the world/
Rita Anya Nara
ISBN: 978-0-9894984-0-1
ISBN-10: 0989498409
1. Travel guidebook 2. Self-help 3. Anxiety disorders 4. Title

Printed in the United States of America

DISCLAIMER

The information presented in this book is the author's personal experience and knowledge gained while traveling, and while completing baccalaureate studies in neurochemistry, toxicology, and human health. The author is not a doctor, but a long-time sufferer of several anxiety disorders who has overcome the limitations of these disorders by journeying some 19,546 miles around the face of the earth. No part of this text should be construed or used as formal medical advice. Consult with your psychiatrist before attempting to travel. While the author strives to make the information herein as timely and accurate as possible, the author makes no promises or guarantees about the completeness, accuracy, or adequacy of the contents of this book, and expressly disclaims liability for errors and omissions. The author shall not be held responsible for any loss or damages resulting from the use of information presented in this book.

DEDICATION

For my sister Christine, who never stopped
encouraging me to try something new and different;
for my father Paul, who never doubted my
determination to take on the world;
and for my mother Mary, my very first travel
companion, and precious friend.

CONTENTS

ACKNOWLEDGMENT

The author would like to acknowledge the UC Davis Pharmacology and Toxicology Program and Dr. Robert P. Diamond for their instrumental role in shaping this book.

CHAPTER 1

Traveling with Anxiety

Anxiety is sometimes referred to as an "illness of lost opportunities." Unlike many other psychiatric problems, where sufferers have lost the will, interest, or capacity to do something, you *want* to do something in your life, but your fears are stopping you. You want to travel and can have everything lined up: time, money, choice of locale, dream itinerary – but your anxiety is preventing you from stepping out the door. Is this heartbreaking? Yes. Is it something you can overcome? Of course. Knowledge, readiness, and the right mindset are going to come through for you even though you know you're not the "ideal" traveler. There *is* no ideal traveler – only a prepared and determined one.

It's true that as an anxiety sufferer you have additional things to be prepared for before going abroad. You need to understand more about the medical resources at a particular place; you need to anticipate and accommodate anxiety triggers that come with various activities; and you need to have back-up plans. And since treatment for an anxiety or panic attack typically involves 1) taking anti-anxiety medications, 2) finding a place to rest and recover, 3) treating physical manifestations, and 4) consulting with a doctor, you need to be prepared to do these things *anywhere, at any time.* You'll learn how to do all of this in the chapters to come.

In this chapter, we'll look at real and perceived barriers to travel, how to overcome them, and why people with anxiety disorders can make great travelers. We'll review the five essential things you need to travel with an anxiety disorder, and explore the all-important question of who to travel with – or if you feel better able to handle the challenge alone. You'll evaluate your own readiness to go abroad, and understand that travel isn't the goal of successful therapy; it *is* your therapy.

Why Do People with Anxiety Want to Travel?

As soon as you step into another country, anything and just about everything can happen. You are surrounded by unknowns: who and what is around you, how things work, and why things are the way they are. You don't know how you'll be perceived or treated, or if you'll be understood. There are the typical things to worry about that plague popular places everywhere: crime, reckless drivers, con artists, freak accidents, congestion, detours, and service cancellations or delays. Then there's the media coverage of catastrophes that have a 0.0001% probability of affecting the average tourist: an embassy bombing, a hotel burning down, or a tour bus crashing into a train – all broadcast with the most vivid images to get your attention.

All this is just what the common traveler has in the back of their mind when they arrive at their destination! You may fear having a panic or anxiety attack in public, incurring expensive medical costs abroad, being ridiculed by insensitive people, running out of pills, buckling under the strain of medication side effects on top of a touring itinerary, or generally having an emotional breakdown. So the burning question becomes:

Why bother?!

If you're so anxious and scared, and have that much to worry about, then why do you want to travel?

The answer is simple: because people with anxiety disorders are explorers. Adventurers. Connoisseurs and sightseers. Wanderers. Trekkers and urbanites. Roamers and nomads, photographers and museum lovers. Journeyers, vagabonds, and sometimes even thrill-seekers. You want what everyone else wants who travels: to relax. To see something different. To treat yourself to something special. To discover new ways of doing or understanding things. To see the bigger picture of human existence. To think about who you are and what you believe in. To remember the simple things in life that bring you the most joy... and so many others.

Besides the common emotional, spiritual, and self-gratifying reasons why people want to travel, here are several that are particularly important to anxiety sufferers.

Being in the moment. At the heart of any anxiety disorder is anticipatory dread of one's circumstances, surroundings, and future – and often, fear of triggering painful memories. The key to managing anxiety when you travel is to understand that being someplace new and different constantly pulls you into your surroundings; you don't have the weight of the future and past

11

bearing down on you simultaneously. As you process things in real time, you see them for what they are; your fear can't distort them. And if you are facing something challenging, you're capable of handling it because you're not wasting energy on repetitive cycles of fear.

Getting out of your mind and back into the present is one of the best things you can do for your anxiety.

Personal development. Since you've already succeeded in managing many aspects of your anxiety in your day-to-day life, you want to take the "next step" by trying bolder things, including travel. You know that traveling can help you evolve in many ways: making you a stronger and more resilient person, helping you become more resourceful and well-rounded, and giving you the confidence to take on new challenges in your personal or professional life. To put it simply, there's nothing like expanding your horizons – literally *and* figuratively.

Questioning. As someone with an anxiety disorder, you may have spent a lot of time thinking about how you fit into the world – often because you've felt like you don't fit in at all. Being a tourist, and not "just" an anxiety sufferer, puts you in a more objective role of exploring and understanding your place in the universe and comparing your life to the lives of others.

Rebellion. Yes, part of wanting to travel is about rebellion: daring to do what people have implied (or flat out told you) that you're not psychologically able to handle. This rebellion can also be against a more frightened version of yourself. Either way, you may feel that you're defying convention by breaking the barriers of your long-established personal limits.

Awakening. Traveling can push you to a new level of consciousness unlike anything else. By being in different places and trying new things around (or with) other people, you may uncover parts of yourself that have long been hidden behind the fear of anxiety. You can discover aspects of your personality, as well as deeper wishes for your life, that you weren't even aware of.

Reassessment. As you see a wider world and your role (and potential role) in it, you may reevaluate how you live, what you want, and what you believe in. Once you get a fresh view of the quality of life possible for yourself, you see clearly the changes you want to make when you return home that will promote your emotional, mental, and physical health.

Think about and list your own reasons for wanting to travel:

_____

_____

_____

Typical Barriers to Traveling with Anxiety, and How to Overcome Them

So how do you deal with the doubts, unknowns, and challenges that come with planning and taking an international trip? The first step is to recognize the real and perceived barriers that are directly or indirectly caused by anxiety. Here are three of the most common.

Being unprepared. Travel insurance studies show that psychiatric problems are among the top five reasons for cutting a trip short (along with things like injuries and cardiovascular diseases). Why? Because people with anxiety disorders often don't know how to tailor a trip to their comfort level, and where to get all the information they need. How do you know what to choose, where to go for help, and what variables, exceptions, and possibilities exist "out there" that will affect your well-being? You wouldn't be reading this book if you already had all those answers.

Cutting a trip short means a person couldn't find the psychiatric care they needed where they were at. Psychiatrists, medical clinics, and pharmacies exist in every country around the world; yes, they're a whole lot easier to find in some places than others, but by doing the right research before your trip, you *can* find what you need abroad to avoid coming home early. You can also anticipate and learn how to manage numerous anxiety triggers and stressful scenarios before you've even landed.

Being unfamiliar and out of practice. You may have traveled ten or twenty years ago, before you were diagnosed with your disorder, and are unsure of how you'll respond now to the excitement and challenges of travel. You may also be unsure of how travel has changed, post-9/11, and how the internet has transformed how people get around. While anti-terrorist measures will affect you for about twenty minutes, tops, on either end of a plane ride, technology's impact on travel is more far-reaching and is discussed frequently throughout this book.

Having the wrong perception. It's important to understand that travel is an activity; it's not a joy ride through the pages of National Geographic, or a daydream with some hotels and cars thrown in to get you around. I don't say this to insult your intelligence, but to emphasize that travel is first and foremost a physical endeavor – a matter of getting yourself from here to there, and working with time, space, and energy to make things happen. It's when you get yourself to a place that your mind and heart can truly take off.

With all this being said, here are the five things you need to be able to travel successfully with an anxiety disorder.

> *I. KNOWLEDGE.* This includes understanding what to do, when – and where, and how. It sounds simple, but it is highly situational. You build your practical knowledge of how best to tour by reading this book, and by traveling.
>
> The other aspect to this, of course, is knowing yourself and your own tolerance for stress. Arguably the biggest reason that people have anxiety or panic attacks is because they've reached their breaking point. Only you really know what this point is; what you may not be aware of are all the ways you can avoid wearing yourself down emotionally, mentally, and physically.
>
> *II. PRACTICE.* Learning how to travel well takes a few tries; you need to not only look at past trips and understand what you learned about yourself and how the world works, but you should take smaller trips

before a large, international trip in order to get into the groove of traveling. Practice leads to experience, and good experiences build confidence while bad experiences always offer something to learn from.

III. DETERMINATION. This is, quite simply, about not giving up, of being able to hold out through more ups and downs on your journey than you might be comfortable with at first. Recognizing stress factors, managing anxiety triggers, and getting through an anxiety or panic attack when you least expect one will require persevering through some unpleasant days. Determination requires stamina, but ultimately rides on willpower. You're the one who decides if the joy that comes with your trip outweighs the challenges.

IV. PLANNING. Like any activity, travel requires arrangements, decisions, and preparations. You may have tried to plan a trip in the past, but did not find planning methods and strategies that took into account emotional health, energy level, phobias, and other elements that specifically affect anxiety sufferers.

V. CONTINGENCIES. Anxiety is rooted in uncertainty about the future and the unfamiliar. Having a back-up plan to manage this uncertainty isn't catering to your anxiety; it's adjusting for it. People have lots of names for contingencies: buffers, safeguards, plans for the unplanned – whatever the case, they require a way of thinking and placing yourself in a given scenario to identify your options and how to protect your mental and emotional health. Contingencies include having a second phone number for your doctor, a digital scan of your passport, a more detailed map, the address of a back-up pharmacy, and many other practical fallbacks that quickly drain the fear and stress out of your plans.

Everything in this book will build on these five concepts.

Why Anxious People Can Make Great Travelers

There are some surprising reasons why people with anxiety disorders can not only manage to take a trip abroad, but – when prepared and confident – make better travelers than the average person. You should recognize characteristics and qualities of yourself in the following.

Informed and insightful. Anxiety sufferers have often spent many years as armchair travelers – reading, watching, and absorbing an enormous amount of information about places and their people. Your understanding of geography, languages, and socio-political events can prove invaluable and advantageous, and give you a great appreciation for what you see compared to someone who lands in a country knowing little more than their credit card limit.

Practical and sensible. Because disorder and uncertainty tend to cause a lot of stress, you're more likely than the average traveler to have everything you need, where you need it, as well as have extra cash, plenty of maps, and a good sense for the drawbacks of what you try or where you go. Don't let anyone tell you that this is the "wrong" way to travel. It's the people who are careful with their security and health abroad, and better equipped to handle problems, who will be successful; the laid-back travelers who are "winging it" are the ones at higher risk.

Perceptive and sensitive. People with anxiety are affected more by trauma than others; however, this sensitivity enables them to appreciate and enjoy the finer details of places and experiences. Anxious people also tend to be highly intelligent and insightful, able to clue into cultural nuances and social norms, and able to avoid creating offense. These qualities are often highly appreciated by the hosts of your foreign country, and can make your interactions much easier.

Resolute. Because a trip may not have turned out well in the past, people with anxiety disorders often have something to prove to themselves; they're less likely to throw their hands up in the air or grind to a halt in the face of a delay or setback. In other words, you've been waiting a while to travel, and you want to do it right; otherwise, you wouldn't be reading this book.

Adaptable. To avoid anxiety and the pain that comes with it, you may have spent a good portion of your life working *around* problems rather than *through* them, and adjusting to uncomfortable circumstances the best way you can. While conformists might disapprove of your approach, the fact remains that you've developed a lot of creativity and resourcefulness from years of self-preservation. These qualities and thought patterns can help you maneuver your way around a travel glitch.

If reading all of this makes you excited to travel, then you are well on your way! Here are some additional questions to ask yourself about your future journey.

My idea of a great vacation is focused on *(for example, sightseeing, relaxing, indulging myself, pushing my own limits, etc.):*

_____

_____

I would most like to:

_____

_____

_____

What I most fear is:

_____

_____

_____

From Armchair to Plane Seat: A Journey to the Other Side of the Horizon

As you start the inner journey that will lead to your international journey, I'll tell you a little about myself and how I got from armchair to plane seat, so to speak.

I grew up in Sacramento, California, which is about a two-hour road trip from San Francisco. Even though Sacramentans are proud of their beautiful city, most people will readily admit that it's overshadowed by its Bay Area sister – one of those stunning, ethereal places that stirs the imagination and tugs the wanderlust heartstrings of people near and far. You don't have to be very old in Sacramento to be told that the grass is greener and the sky is bluer in *San Francisco*. When I first visited, I'm sure it was filled with as many scumbags and pickpockets as any other city, but all I saw was a fairytale land of beauty, with surprises and mysteries up and down every hill.

Then, of course, there was the magic of visiting the ocean for the first time. As if my mind wasn't already drifting many miles away, my father told me that the water at my feet was going to wash up next on the shores of the other side of the planet. Places like China. Japan. Can you possibly feel so close, but so far from these mega-exotic enigmas than being nine years old and standing in the tide of the Pacific Ocean? And what else was "just on the other side" of all that water?

By ten years old I'd read every book on China and Japan in my school library, and soon after, every other book on a foreign country. By twelve I was toting travel phrase books to lunch, bed, my favorite armchair, and lots of places in between. For better or worse, "my" places and "my" languages distracted me from my extreme shyness and sensitivity to those walking, talking riddles around me called *human beings*. I experienced my first panic attack at thirteen, and by fifteen I had developed anorexia, social anxiety, and a severe case of obsessive-compulsive disorder. I used my later teen years to bring most of these problems under control, and recognize that I needed to "be careful" to stop aggravating a genetic predisposition for anxiety. "Being careful" took many forms for me, and in any case, I put away my spinning globe for years.

In 2000, at the age of 22, I graduated at the top of my class after completing baccalaureate studies in toxicology and neurochemistry. Almost immediately after, I landed a job that I liked, and – thanks to having worked part-time while I was a student – I didn't have a dime of debt. This was all great, but I was a wreck: over four years I'd been on and off five different anti-anxiety medications and a couple of anti-depressants, and I'd resisted my psychiatrist's suggestions of behavioral therapy. After suffering what I'd call a moderate breakdown, I decided to take a four-day vacation – a trip to Vancouver, Canada.

Unfortunately, I didn't know how to do much of anything: make a hotel reservation, check out of a room, or rent a car. I was convinced I couldn't use my Visa card outside of the United States, so I brought a ton of cash with me, and I showed up north of the border with no passport and a large can of pepper spray in my purse. It was a good thing my mother was with me the whole time, because Canadian Customs was not happy with me. Still, the trip went without a major hitch, and I was hooked on travel – again.

The terrorist attacks of 9/11 barely put a dent in my desire to tour the countryside. I stayed in North America – mainly because I was still a little afraid, and still trying to find the right medication and treatment – but even so, I was amazed at what I was able to do with a little experience, quite a bit of planning, and a lot of determination. Less than three years after arriving like a fool in Vancouver, I took a 2,100 mile dream road trip across Quebec and Ontario, and in 2006 – even though I didn't go much of anywhere – I worked up the nerve to list every country and city I wanted to see over the next ten years. Finally, in 2009, with my medications stabilized, I decided to brave my way to New Zealand, alone. Although I got sick during the trip, and made some mistakes, I learned from them and knew I was ready for the next step.

A year later I was walking my luggage up the national highway of Iceland while a certain infamous volcano named Eyjafjallajökull blew nearby. I wasn't supposed to be on that highway, or even in the country; Iceland's transportation system was in a state of disarray, and it would be even harder for me to get a flight out of there than it had been to circle around the volcanic ash to get in. Was all this exciting? Yes. Terrifying? No. And so you'll ask, why? Because I was *in the moment.* All my mental, physical, and emotional energy was focused on the twenty feet just in front of me. Everything I really needed to manage my anxiety disorder was either in my purse, my heart, or my mind. I was both bold and cautious; prepared and spontaneous. And I was relaxed. My anxiety didn't stand a chance of taking me down.

Despite eight major plane, bus, and train detours in the coming weeks across Northern Europe, I used all my wits and guts to traverse five more countries on that trip, and I came home in better mental and emotional shape than I'd left. After that, I built my life around a major international trip every few months, and I collected experiences like the sky soaking up a rainbow. In early 2013, when I landed in Paradise Bay, Antarctica, I achieved a life-long dream of journeying to all seven continents on earth.

Did it take a long time and a lot of determination to make it that far? Absolutely – and I didn't always have the energy, time, or will to travel. Like many people, I was busy doing other things: I wrote and sold articles and travel essays, I became a photographer, I became a hiker... and I had more panic attacks, including one in 2007 that left me in the hospital. All the while my psychiatrist encouraged me to push my limits – just beyond the point that I was comfortable, and never to the point that I was overwhelmed – and reminded me of how much I liked going to "the other side of the horizon." Although sometimes I regret not traveling more in my late twenties, I'm also grateful for that "relapse" to armchair traveler because it made me think about everything I'd learned and discovered, and how I could see and do so much more. And when I finally got moving again, I realized I'd developed an innate sense for when I was too fragile to leave a hotel room, and when backing off was more important than cancellation fees or schedules.

The more I mastered balancing my needs for adventure and psychological safety, the more I realized that I couldn't be stopped – figuratively, anyway. In the fall of 2012, a train breakdown in an isolated forest of southwest Poland was the latest challenge thrown my way. As most of the fifty or so other passengers stayed at their seats cursing our conductor for running the A/C too hard, I went for a walk nearby. I wasn't worried; I had enough stamina, pills, water, patience, experience, local currency, and mystery-flavored Belarusian-brand energy bars to last me through a night. To put it simply, I knew I was going to be alright. In fact, I felt a little giddy, and silly. As I went through one of my bags in search of those energy bars, I realized:

I've gone from head-case to suitcase.

Yes, I gave myself a good laugh, and when I thought back to the train escapade on my flight home to San Francisco, my journey *from armchair to plane seat* definitely sounded better. It became the inspiration for a great book I wanted to write. And so I'm sharing my knowledge and experience with you, knowing that you're worried about countless things: how medication side effects can impact travel. How to overcome jet lag and exhaustion. How people from drastically different cultures perceive and respond to "head-cases." You may not know how to enjoy yourself and sightsee while maneuvering crowds and distractions, or how you would find a reputable pharmacist in another country if something happened to your pills on the road. You may think that travel means discomfort, sleep deprivation, mental and emotional overload, and just plain too much stress to make it all worth it. And yet you *know* it's worth it, because you've been to "the other side of the horizon" before, at some time. You're just dreaming of a bigger journey, and you don't want to be held back any longer. Here's the great news:

**The most amazing experience awaits you,
because travel *is* therapy, and the world,
quite literally, is where you will overcome
your fears and the limitations of your anxiety disorder.**

Travelers always think in terms of getting from "here" to "there." Think like a traveler, except on an emotional level: recognize where you're at today, and where you want to end up. You can go from fearful to brave, foolish to smart, clueless to savvy, and many other "states." So where do you want to get to?

I want to go from _____ *to* _____.

Self-Assessment: Being Ready to Travel

Once you've made the decision to travel, consider the following.

What's changed since the last major trip you took?

_____

_____

_____

_____

_____

What is your doctor going to think of your idea?

_____

_____

_____

_____

How will your family and friends react? Will they be scared for you? Excited for you? Why?

_____

_____

_____

_____

_____

Who to Travel With

Chapter 5 will help you make a lot of decisions about where you go and what you do on a trip. Who you travel with – if anyone – is something you should think about even before narrowing down a list of countries or crafting a proposed itinerary. One of the reasons is practical – to introduce someone to your idea of traveling together, or to start looking at available group tours – while the other is an acknowledgment of the importance of this decision. For better or worse, it's who you're with in life that can make all the difference in the world.

Your list of potential travel companions may require a lot of thought since your social or familial landscape, level of independence, and economic status may have been drastically different the last time you took a vacation. Some of the decision also depends on your personality, and whether the activities you're interested in require two or more people. Of course, after reading this section and thinking about the availability and willingness of your family and friends to go abroad, you could decide to look into a Professional Travel Companion (which will be discussed more in Chapter 5), or come to the conclusion that you're ready to go it alone.

TRAVELING WITH FAMILY OR FRIENDS

No two relatives or friends are alike, but the basic concept of traveling with family or friends is the same: experiencing the excitement and challenges of navigating a foreign country with someone else. It's essential that your companion(s) be *both* interested in the place, *and* in discovering it with you. If you've established this, and your companion(s) have the time and money to travel, then consider these advantages and disadvantages of touring with family or friends.

Understanding of your condition. Being who they are, family and friends know that you have an anxiety disorder and need to take medication, and have most likely seen you both suffer and recover from an attack. They can be crucial in getting you your pills, to your hotel room, or to a doctor during an anxiety or panic attack. They may also shield you from unwanted attention from strangers, and monitor your recovery.

Help with difficult things. Family and friends usually know what causes you significant stress, and may readily step in when they see you struggling with your anxiety triggers – either because it's not a big deal for them, or because they want to spare you discomfort. This can be even more valuable if they are experienced travelers, or you're in an extremely different environment.

You can observe how a family member or friend manages a difficult situation until you feel more comfortable trying it yourself.

Resentment. The same person or people you depend on may not have any problems with anxiety themselves, and may grow impatient if you keep pulling them away from activities that they enjoy, but that trigger your anxiety. This problem can intensify if there isn't the time or means for both of you to indulge your own interests and comfort levels on a trip; in some cases, an upset friend or family member might part ways with you mid-vacation, which can be extremely stressful and damage your confidence. Think about how much you're able to keep your frustrations to yourself and make yourself happy, and how tolerant and understanding your potential travel companion is.

Disappointment. Even though they love you, and – for the most part – accept you for who you are, family and friends may expect or hope that you're a "less affected" person on a vacation, i.e., that your anxiety disorder suddenly goes away when you leave home. Finding out otherwise can be disheartening for them, and uncomfortable for you. If you're traveling with a family member and your anxiety is at least partly hereditary, their feelings of disappointment may deepen into guilt and shame.

Less responsibility. Much of the grunt work of travel – watching luggage, asking for directions, buying tickets, and the like – can be split between two or more people. If periodically freeing yourself of having to worry about these things is essential for you, consider the value of the team effort in getting around.

TRAVELING WITH A TOUR GROUP

People who suffer from an anxiety disorder are not necessarily shy or introverted, and may want to be part of a tour group because it will greatly enrich their travel experience. Even if you're not a fan of group travel, traveling with a tour may be the only practical way to visit very remote or ecologically sensitive destinations. There are some key advantages and disadvantages of being "part of the crowd" on a bus, cruise, or expedition when you have an anxiety disorder.

Support network. While they're not your trusted friends, both tour operators and other tour guests are a built-in contingency of people who could help you in the event of an anxiety or panic attack.

Furthermore, tour operators usually have a legal obligation to respond to a medical emergency, and tours often have readier access and transportation to a physician than you could otherwise find on your own or with your private circle.

Shared experience. People with anxiety disorders tend to appreciate a more personal experience of the world, and may resent being part of a "herd" subject to someone else's narration of a place or event. Distancing yourself from the group can restore your sense of individuality and independence, but it may also mean missing the bus back to the hotel, or frustrating your tour guide.

No privacy. Personal space and time to decompress are usually essential for anxiety sufferers, and both could be lacking if your tour runs on a tight schedule and resources are limited. You may find it unnerving to see the same people from dawn to dusk at tourist attractions, across the aisle on the bus, down the hotel hallway, and finally, in the hotel sauna when you're just trying to reconnect with yourself.

Pacing. You generally can't move much faster than the overall group, which can be good if you're worried about overdoing it and exhausting yourself. Conversely, a group can lift you up and get you going if anxiety is adversely affecting your energy level.

Feelings of isolation. If you're among a lot of relaxed, talkative travelers who decidedly don't suffer from anxiety, you could feel dejected and spend a lot of time wondering how and why they aren't affected by certain things the way you are.

TRAVELING ALONE

Traveling on your own is a unique experience, and can be very rewarding despite a few drawbacks. Going it alone may sound like a potential disaster for someone with an anxiety disorder, but I can attest to traveling through dozens of countries on my own and returning home more confident, relaxed, and inspired by my physical and psychological journey than I could have ever dreamed. It may not be the best way to *start out* traveling, but if you're an introvert and your travel goals exceed the ambitions of family or friends, it may be the way you end up truly "taking off." Here are some things to consider.

Empowerment. You can take tremendous pride in your own abilities and efforts when you go it alone. You'll build your confidence more rapidly, and recognize and work on your shortcomings as a traveler faster than if you were depending on others to do things for you.

Less pressure. If you need to lie around your hotel room, or on the beach for an entire day because you feel overwhelmed or just need to unwind, there's no one to explain yourself to, and no one to inconvenience or disappoint.

Fears about safety. Anxious people are prone to distraction or disconnection from their surroundings (including people) as a self-defense mechanism. You should recognize that although technological advancements including cell phones and personal alarms have made it safer than ever to travel alone, your vigilance doesn't come with an on or off button – it requires a level of consciousness that will pull some of your energy from sightseeing (at least until it becomes instinctive).

One of the biggest safety concerns, of course, is traveling alone as a woman, particularly if you are under forty. Rape, assault, kidnap, and murder are ghastly things to think of when about half the people at the places you want to explore are stronger than you. I haven't been assaulted abroad, so I'm not qualified to speak on the matter. There are at least a dozen books out there on how to travel safely as a woman, so if you don't want to rely on your own street smarts, try reading one of them.

Loneliness. Even people with severe social anxiety can long for someone to talk to or connect with after a long day of sightseeing alone. If you don't have someone to call, email, or skype at the end of the day, consider how you will manage feelings of isolation and loneliness. If there really is no one back home to call, then try writing a postcard to someone who won't expect it, or posting the day's travel photos to the internet for coworkers to enjoy. Another idea is to stay at a Bed and Breakfast or a hostel instead of a hotel, so you'll at least be around (if not with) more people.

Potential to drink. Alcohol may look magnitudes more tempting when it's served at exotic little hideaways that are open all night, and there's no one you know to notice you dropping in. Many anxiety sufferers generally can't and don't drink because most anti-anxiety medications have contraindications with alcohol, but your ability to stay away can be compromised if you're on your own and want to take "forgetting your disorder" to the next level by skipping your meds for a large glass of wine. If you're worried about being tempted, try asking the hotel receptionist about the worst bar in the entire city, and let the stories dampen your desire. If you still think it could be a major problem, consider a travel companion – one who doesn't drink.

Self-awareness. Being alone generally means that you're better tuned in to your mind, body, and emotions – which is not always a good thing, but can help you more readily recognize when you're exhausted and need to scale back your activities to prevent an anxiety attack. Consider how being around others may have distracted you from your own warning signs in the past, and factor it into your decision of how to travel.

Whether you choose to travel on your own or with others, you are responsible for your own happiness – and for staying determined to see your dream journey through.

CHAPTER 2

A Brief Look at Anxiety, How it is Treated, and Travel

Anxiety often develops as a result of several factors: your experiences in life, neurochemical imbalance, personality, and genetic predisposition. While all distinct, the four most common disorders – panic disorder, social anxiety disorder, post-traumatic stress disorder, and generalized anxiety disorder – present similar challenges to planning and successfully taking a major trip. Which disorder you suffer from will influence what you choose to see and do, with whom, and how. The important thing to remember is that any anxiety disorder can be successfully managed so that you can travel abroad.

The medications used to treat anxiety come from a growing number of classes, including selective serotonin reuptake inhibitors (SSRIs such as Zoloft, Prozac, and Paxil); serotonin-norepinephrine reuptake inhibitors (SNRIs such as Cymbalta and Effexor); azapirones (such as BuSpar); and benzodiazepines (Xanax and Valium). In this chapter we'll look at how the typical side effects of these medications can affect you as a traveler. We'll also look at the classical elements of Cognitive Behavioral Therapy and how they correlate to the activity of traveling.

Bipolar disorder (manic depression) and generalized depression, which can also have a considerable impact on travel, are both mood disorders; the particular challenges they present are addressed in Chapter 9. Anxiety disorders including obsessive-compulsive disorder (OCD) and seasonal affective disorder (SAD) are also specifically addressed in that chapter.

Panic Disorder

Panic disorder is characterized by recurring, severe panic attacks, which are sudden-onset periods of intense fear that can last from minutes to hours. Symptoms can include trembling, shortness of breath or hyperventilation, heart palpitations, chest pain or tightness, sweating, burning sensations, dizziness and lightheadedness, sensations of choking, and difficulty moving. In short, you can feel entirely incapacitated during a panic attack. Complications arise during travel since manifestations can be misinterpreted by strangers as another type of health emergency, and you could be unable to communicate your needs.

Panic disorder is frequently unpredictable, adding to concern about its impact on your plans, your psychological health, and even your safety. If you've suffered from panic disorder for a while, you may be able to tell earlier than you used to if you feel "off" and an attack is imminent. Recognizing your own subtle warning signs can help you avoid (but not always prevent) aggravating triggers that lead to an attack, and help you salvage a significant portion of your trip.

Besides doing this, there are a couple of attack symptoms you may want to focus on controlling over others. Becoming paralyzed with fear (i.e., unable to move), and being unable to speak are the most damaging manifestations abroad because they could impact your safety and well-being. This isn't just if you're near a roadway or other hazard when you start to exhibit severe symptoms; unfortunately, people who are incapacitated can be taken advantage of or violated in quiet areas, and even in public. You may want to talk to your psychiatrist, as well as a behavioral therapist, about how you can stay responsive even as you suffer significant physical symptoms.

Social Anxiety

Social anxiety disorder (SAD, or SAnD to avoid confusion with seasonal affective disorder) is characterized by an intense fear of interpersonal situations that can adversely affect your decisions, activities, and well-being. Symptoms include trembling, sweating, heart palpitations, stammering and rapid speech, and nausea when interacting (or even thinking of interacting) with others.

Some sufferers are more sensitive to strangers, while others experience stress around those they are loosely acquainted with (e.g., a hotel receptionist you see every day whose curiosity and attention sends you reeling). Others may fear interacting with people in certain positions, such as taxi drivers or aggressive salespeople. Your particular sensitization can influence a number of the choices you make in planning and taking a trip. You are less likely to be bothered by certain places or events than someone who suffers from panic disorder or post-traumatic stress disorder; you also may be far more ambitious and confident than the average person when it comes to taking on a challenging itinerary or an adventure travel expedition alone.

If you don't automatically decide to travel alone, then you're likely to avoid group tours and travel with a trusted companion instead – although such a companion might not be easy to find, or comfortable to have along, depending on the extent to which social anxiety disorder has affected your daily life. Whether you find a companion or not, you can dispel a lot of your anxiety over social interactions by recognizing which aspects of these interactions you can control, as well as the different roles you play as a tourist and how to be comfortable in them. Chapter 6 goes into detail on this subject.

Post-Traumatic Stress Disorder (PTSD)

PTSD can develop after an event, such as personal assault or the violent death of a loved one, that results in significant psychological trauma. Symptoms include re-experiencing the original trauma through flashbacks or nightmares, and avoidance of places, things, and other reminders of the event. Sufferers may have difficulty staying or falling asleep, experience prolonged anger, and may be hypervigilant of their surroundings. These manifestations can make it difficult to enjoy a trip, or to even move forward with some parts of your journey.

Because PTSD is highly situational, as well as unpredictable, you might sit down and start eliminating large numbers of places or activities that you think may aggravate memories of a traumatic incident. While certain sights, sounds, and even smells in an unfamiliar environment can stir feelings of extreme anxiety, PTSD sufferers generally experience far less stress around people (including strangers) than other anxiety sufferers. If this holds true for you, then consider how being around others (such as on a group tour) can actually mitigate your triggers. Sharing a more common perspective can help you experience something that is usually threatening in a more benign context.

If a tour is not your thing, then traveling with a trusted companion can also help keep you focused on the big picture around you.

Generalized Anxiety

Generalized anxiety disorder (GAD) is characterized by uncontrollable and excessive worry that interferes with your overall daily functioning. You may fixate on dozens (and sometimes hundreds) of "what ifs" that others don't even notice or consider. GAD manifestations include restlessness, fatigue, muscle tension, fidgeting, headaches, difficulty concentrating, irritability, insomnia, and trembling.

When you have GAD, the number of stimuli, variables, and potential complications involved in traveling can seem overwhelming, to the point of seeming ridiculous to even take on. What many sufferers don't realize is that all the mental energy spent worrying about family and friendship problems, work difficulties, money, health issues, death, larger life issues, and just about everything in between can be diverted to more pleasurable things when accompanied by a dramatic change in surroundings.

Because GAD sufferers typically anticipate negative experiences, setbacks, and sometimes nothing short of disaster, building a number of positive experiences is often the most powerful way to change your thought patterns. More than other anxiety sufferers, you may consider a series of shorter, smaller trips before taking a larger trip in order to understand the challenges of travel and which cause you significant dysfunction. The latter can then be divided into those you'd like to avoid for now, and those you feel you could work through.

Phobias

A phobia is an intense fear of something that may (but doesn't necessarily) pose little or no actual danger. Phobias are closely connected to anxiety; they're among (or involved with) the most common triggers of anxiety or panic attacks. Some of the phobias aggravated by travel include:

- Fear of crowded places;
- Fear of germs;
- Fear of flying; and
- Fear of strangers.

Phobias are the shape-shifters on the anxiety landscape because they form and subside depending on your experiences. The more positive experiences you have with something you're afraid of, the less powerful your phobia becomes. Of course, you have to work up the courage to confront something before you can have a positive experience. The key to doing this is to not overwhelm yourself. You can often manage many phobias at once by confronting one or two at a time. For example, if you have all of the phobias listed above, then you could pick a flight that departs at mid-day (when the airport is less crowded, with fewer people, and fewer germs). If your journey is like 99.99% of all flights, then it will be without incident – and your fear has lost more of its legitimacy.

Now that we've taken a brief look at anxiety disorders and phobias, let's look at how to address complications posed by the medications used to treat them.

How Medication Side Effects Can Impact Travel

As a society and a civilization, we've generally accepted that the benefits of taking medications greatly outweigh the drawbacks. Those drawbacks usually present themselves as side effects – unwanted physiological consequences of using a medication. Many side effects reduce in intensity once you've been taking a drug for a while, but others can still be bothersome; you either get used to them, or not. During travel, some side effects are going to be more disruptive than others, while others that you normally notice can seem to disappear.

It's important to understand that both internal and external factors can affect how you experience side effects when you're in a dramatically different environment (namely, when you are traveling). Travel companions are not necessarily going to understand or help you address these, especially given the number of people who seem to think that all medications 1) make you drowsy, and 2) give you an upset stomach (and not a whole lot more). Spikes in adrenaline, altered levels of other hormones, jet lag, and other factors can influence how you think, react, and feel on your trip. Try making a special appointment with your psychiatrist to anticipate how you will be able to:

1. Recognize and distinguish your side effects from travel problems such as dehydration, diarrhea, and travel fatigue; and

2. Travel in order to not exacerbate your side effects.

Below are eighteen of the most frequently experienced side effects of taking anti-anxiety medications, loosely grouped by the physiological function or system affected. Pick out the ones that impact you, and take some time to address them individually.

Drowsiness. One of the most common side effects, drowsiness can affect your ability to stay alert throughout even the most enjoyable and stimulating days. If you're like many people, you have a nap (or even two) built into your daily schedule to manage drowsiness (you may or may not sleep during this time, since drowsiness is not the same as sleepiness). Travel can easily throw off this napping/resting schedule, so strategize with your doctor about how you can build downtime into your tour days.

Sleep disruption. This side effect can be exacerbated by any number of things during a trip, including jet lag, noisy neighbors at your place of lodging, stomach upset from eating unfamiliar food, and travel fatigue. All of these issues, and how to manage them, are addressed in this book.

Insomnia. Doctors will usually tell you that the most natural fix for insomnia is physical activity. If you already suffer from insomnia, then scheduling long bus tours and other itineraries that involve little or no physical activity is not recommended. You should also be careful not to eat out only an hour or two before you expect to fall asleep.

Vivid dreaming. This side effect is more prevalent with the use of recently developed anti-anxiety medications, and it can intensify when you travel since, as we sleep, the brain tries to process emotional and mental experiences our mind couldn't fully resolve during the day. How much you're affected depends on your sleep quality and the type of sleep you experience (deep sleep, REM sleep, etc.), which may differ abroad due to various environmental factors. Of course, vivid dreaming is not actually a negative experience for many people.

Fatigue. Any normal fatigue you experience as a result of taking medications will be compounded the first couple of days that you travel (particularly when combined with jet lag), but may rapidly subside as you grow used to the pace of your trip. Several of the travel decisions that directly and indirectly impact fatigue are discussed in Chapter 5.

Dizziness and lightheadedness. Not surprisingly, these side effects will affect you during transportation the most. You should also be aware that many motion sickness medications, including those sold over-the-counter, can make you lightheaded. Other aggravations include ventilation problems and air quality issues that plague many large cities, trains, and buses; these problems are greatly exacerbated by touring during rush hours. Many of the choices you can make about getting around on your trip are discussed in Chapter 7.

Unsteadiness and impaired coordination may pose more of a confidence issue than a threat to your physical well-being, depending on their severity and the level of activity you're planning. You'll need to pay particular attention to any time you change activities and energy levels, such as getting off a plane after a long flight, or carrying your luggage down hotel stairs ten minutes after waking up.

To identify when and where this side effect may pose a particular problem, have someone (your doctor, or a loved one with some travel experience) read your planned itinerary. What might seem reasonable to you (or something you may have overlooked) might raise a red flag to others, such as going skiing right after a long, winding bus ride.

Difficulty concentrating. This is one of those side effects that may decrease during travel, particularly if one of the reasons you're taking a trip is to get away from a mentally exhausting job, or stagnation in your life. Concentration problems may crop up if you need to process sudden bursts of information (such as complicated directions or instructions) or devise an alternative travel or navigation plan on short notice. Chapter 6 contains information on managing problems with concentration and poor memory.

Depression. If you've already booked or are scheduling a trip, then you've already won half the battle against a relatively infrequent, but significant, side effect. We'll talk more in Chapter 9 about strategies and activities for combating depression once you're traveling.

Irritability. It's often difficult to understand why some medications cause feelings of antagonism and aggravation, other than to acknowledge that no pharmaceutical compound is going to interact 100% perfectly with your brain chemistry. As a side effect, irritability can be toxic when combined with travel setbacks, accidents, or mistakes. Careful planning, and ditching expectations of perfection are critical to preventing escalation of stress and anger. This book will arm you with dozens of effective planning techniques; your personal expectations are up to you.

Tremor and restlessness. These side effects may be something others notice more than you do. Mild shaking and excessive fidgeting can manifest themselves even when you feel calm and relaxed. If these things don't interfere with your well-being, then don't let them bother you. Be aware, though, that they can affect how others perceive you, and can sometimes put service personnel or fellow passengers on edge.

Nausea. Unfortunately, this side effect can be aggravated by any number of things during travel, including what and how much you eat and drink, how you get around, and environmental factors such as air quality. Some of the best things you can do are to pick an upset-stomach medication that also treats nausea; give yourself a break between plane, train, bus, and taxi rides; and keep a regular eye out for ventilation problems.

Muscle cramps. This side effect is often alleviated by the increased amount of walking and other physical activity you usually get when traveling. If you're especially active, you may not notice it at all during your trip.

Headache. Be aware of when and how much you normally experience a headache as a result of taking medications. A headache is a significant indicator of common travel problems such as dehydration and poor ventilation, both of which should be addressed early to avoid getting worse.

Asthenia (weakness or lack of bodily strength). People generally experience an increase in adrenaline when they travel, caused by anticipation, eagerness, and other positive emotions. This adrenaline is often enough to overcome many of the typical manifestations of asthenia, so that you may feel much stronger and more resilient than normal. You'll need to be careful not to overdo it since your muscles won't be used to the extra work, and you could injure yourself.

Dry mouth. This is a benign but irritating problem that will be exacerbated by airplane and train travel. Bringing some hard candy to suck on during the ride can go a long way in dealing with it.

Constipation. Like dry mouth, constipation is another of those side effects that's more of a nuisance than a challenge. It can be compounded by dehydration and by eating the convenience foods that are far more accessible than fresh food during travel. Fortunately, over-the-counter remedies rarely interact with anti-anxiety medications, and Metamucil is as common abroad as

McDonald's.

Diarrhea. It's very important to understand how much you normally suffer from diarrhea as a side effect, so that you can identify when you've actually consumed unsafe food or unclean water abroad. Pay attention to whether your side effect occurs on an empty or full stomach, and how it corresponds to your dosing schedule.

Common travel problems such as diarrhea, dehydration, and travel fatigue will be discussed in detail in the next chapter.

Cognitive Behavioral Therapy in the Real World (i.e., Travel)

Cognitive Behavioral Therapy (CBT) has been effective in the treatment of many anxiety disorders, and is often considered an essential accompaniment to pharmaceutical treatment. It focuses on exposure to the things that cause you anxiety – in a structured, controlled environment. Because of CBT's perceived concentration on hypothetical elements, and the "controlled environment," it's not necessarily popular; while there's no denying that it's relevant to your daily life, it's not necessarily going to help with what you want to try in the future: travel.

In general, CBT is broken down into six phases:

1. **Assessment;**

2. **Reconceptualization;**

3. **Acquiring skills;**

4. **Developing adaptive coping strategies;**

5. **Generalization and maintenance;** and

6. **Post-treatment assessment follow-up.**

Let's admit it: this is some heady, abstract stuff. Since you are reading this book, you're searching for practical answers and techniques to fulfill a dream of traveling despite your anxiety disorder. We established in the first chapter that travel doesn't have to be the painstaking reward of long hours of therapy; it *is* therapy. How each phase of CBT correlates to the travel process is summarized below.

1. **Assessment** (recognizing that you want to travel, but that certain fears are holding you back);

2. **Reconceptualization** (understanding that the places, things, activities, and people that cause you anxiety can be managed differently to mitigate your fears);

3. **Acquiring skills** (reading this book, and traveling);

4. **Developing adaptive coping strategies** (applying your knowledge

to respond differently to your environment, and coming to a comfortable compromise between your anxiety and everything around you);

5. **Generalization and maintenance** (understanding what works for you and what doesn't, and what to do about it; applying what you've learned during travel to other parts of your life); and

6. **Post-treatment assessment follow-up** (understanding why some things worked on your trip while others didn't; recognizing what you've accomplished and how you've changed; and continuing to travel).

The rest of this book focuses on giving you the knowledge and strategies to manage and overcome anxiety during all aspects of your trip. As you begin your internal journey, and then your external journey, you'll develop a good sense for what you're ready to confront head-on, and what activities will need more practice, patience, and determination.

CHAPTER 3

The Unique Physical, Mental, and Emotional Challenges of Travel

Few experiences will remind you of how much you're used to standing still, so to speak, than travel. Fortunately, the numerous physiological factors that you'll encounter while getting from "here" to "there" can all be managed. Being determined, having a good attitude, and being in reasonable aerobic fitness are the first steps; awareness and accommodation of the challenges that come with landing and touring thousands of miles away will take you much farther. We'll look at how travel fatigue, altitude, and jet lag can all impact anxiety, and go over practicalities such as managing medication doses among time zones. You'll learn about unanticipated physical contributors to panic attacks such as allergies found in foreign environments, and how to manage dehydration, extreme climates, and other factors that impact your stamina so that you're mentally, physically, and emotionally resilient enough to enjoy a successful trip.

How Jet Lag Impacts Anxiety

Jet lag is a condition resulting from alterations to the body's circadian rhythms caused by trans-meridian (west–east, or east–west) air travel. When traveling across a number of time zones, your body's natural pattern is upset as the cycles that govern times for sleeping, eating, and body temperature regulation no longer correspond to your environment. To the extent that your body cannot immediately realign these rhythms, you are "jet lagged." Symptoms can either aggravate anxiety, or be mistaken for intensified side effects of medications. Some of the most common jet lag symptoms include:

- Headache and irritability;
- Balance and coordination problems;
- Difficulty concentrating;
- Early awakening (if flying west) or trouble falling asleep (if flying east); and
- Interrupted sleep.

Jet lag usually occurs with a change of three time zones or more, and the extent to which you're affected depends on the number of time zones crossed. If you're unfamiliar with jet lag, you might think that the number of hours that your destination is ahead of you is the number of hours you are jetlagged; however, the maximum possible disruption is plus or minus twelve hours. If the time difference between two locations is greater than twelve hours, subtract that number from 24 to understand the "adjusted" time zone difference. New Zealand, for example, being nineteen hours ahead of Pacific Standard Time, would pose only a five-hour jet lag challenge to a traveler from California.

The recovery time for jet leg is generally one day per time zone crossed, although many people (particularly those who travel more) are able to recover faster. Women are affected by jet lag more than men, since normal nighttime and daytime body rhythms are connected to estrogen levels. Recovery will also depend on whether your flight(s) are overnight or scheduled during the day. You'll typically experience more jet lag if you begin a long flight mid-morning or early afternoon than if you take a "red eye" flight departing at eight p.m. or later (it helps, of course, if you can actually fall asleep on an airplane).

Unfortunately, there are no great ways to avoid jet lag. You can talk to your general care practitioner about where specifically you're going, and how to strategize flight times and sleep hours, to try to minimize the impacts. Your doctor may suggest getting only a minimal amount of sleep the night before your flight (so that you're naturally sleepy when you arrive at your destination) or taking a prescription-strength sleep medication for the first several nights of your trip.

Other Health Challenges of Flying, and How to Offset Them

While not a lot can be done to avoid jet lag, some of the other challenges posed by sitting in a tube for a long stretch can be successfully managed.

High blood sugar. Plenty of travelers love to pick on the quality of airplane food and the stinginess with which it's handed out, particularly on shorter flights. While it's true that airlines have cut down on (or now charge for) their food service to save money, I've yet to encounter a trans-ocean flight that didn't include two meals in the ticket price – and this is usually accompanied by one, if not two snack and beverage services, to the point that you may feel downright overfed. The airlines' rationale is that on long flights you'll miss one food service because you are asleep, in the lavatory, etc., and they don't want passengers coming back to the service kitchen after an hour or two complaining that they're hungry.

Unfortunately, eating all the food the airline offers can be far too much sugar, salt, and fat than you need in order to sit for eight to twelve hours in a cramped space. Even if you're able to do some light exercise in the back of the aircraft or in your seat, being relatively confined after eating a full meal (particularly if you eat more when you're nervous) can be a serious anxiety trigger. Think about how much activity you're used to after a moderate to heavy meal, and how fast you can doze off after eating a lot (assuming that you want to nap on the flight). Depending on your self-assessment, cut down on how much you eat of what's served, or refuse a meal service altogether. At the beginning of your flight, ask the flight attendant when meals are served, and decide which one you will skip.

When you book your ticket, many airlines allow you to request low sugar or low sodium meals, but their success in actually serving these tends to suffer once they start making their harried rounds down the aisle. You might check with the airline staff at the flight gate counter to remind them that you've requested special meals (flight attendants usually work the gate counter before they board the plane with you, and will remember you).

Lack of exercise and poor blood circulation. Many people do some sort of stretching or exercise on long flights, and you might find it advantageous to do the same, particularly to ease the muscle tension and restlessness that come with anxiety.

There are three places you can exercise or stretch on a plane:

1. At your seat, particularly if you have an aisle or window seat, or are seated in an emergency exit row, economy plus, or business class. Note that many airlines include muscle relaxation exercises in the back pages of their in-flight magazine. While you may feel self-conscious pushing your arms above your head or doing some leg raises, you can be sure that others are contemplating doing the same thing rather than thinking that you look silly.

2. If you're in a middle seat or are otherwise cramped for space, then you can stretch or exercise in the back of the aircraft, between the lavatories and the flight attendant service kitchen. This is where many people go to stand and stay loose, for anywhere from a couple minutes to thirty minutes or more. Usually the worst embarrassment you'll suffer is a flight attendant or passenger squeezing by you on the way from the galley or the bathroom.

3. If it causes you severe anxiety to stretch or move where others can see you, wait for the line to the bathroom to disappear, and do some exercises in the lavatory. Five

minutes can go a long way towards making you feel better.

If the rear of the plane is occupied with other people trying to stay loose or use the bathroom, and you can hardly move at all in your seat, try some muscle-tensing exercises to tire out (i.e., relax) your muscles. Try holding your arms out in front of you, lifting your thighs for a minute or more at a time, or tensing and then relaxing abdominal and back muscles.

Subtle hyperventilation. Even if you feel relatively relaxed on your flight, you may not be breathing well because of subconscious tension or restricted movement. Normally, when you change positions or get up, you take a nice deep breath, and you're simply not doing this as much (or at all) on a plane. Poor breathing usually means that you're inhaling faster than normal, so not as much air is entering your lungs with each breath. Long hours of fast or shallow breathing can cause dizziness, muscle spasms, lightheadedness, and other physical problems that sacrifice your body's ability to manage stress.

Besides stretching and getting some exercise, practice some deep breathing exercises at your seat. While many people with anxiety find these exercises irritating, pulling more air in and out of your lungs is a means to an end and doesn't have to take long. Also, be aware that in many large airplanes, the ceiling is higher over your head than you may be used to, so don't forget that your air vent is up there; make sure it's open and providing you with comfortable circulation.

Motion sickness. Before your trip, check with your doctor about possible interactions between your anti-anxiety medications and prescription motion sickness medication (usually patches) that you may need. The chances are slim that over-the-counter motion sickness pills like Dramamine or Bonine are going to adversely interact with SSRIs, SNRIs, or benzodiazepines, but again, you might run this by your psychiatrist just to make sure.

If you don't want to deal with more pills, or with patches, try taking ginger to combat motion sickness; many people find it to be an effective treatment. Another option is to wear Sea-Bands, which are specially designed elastic bands with acupressure points worn above the wrists for preventing motion sickness (the technology is based on principles of traditional Chinese medicine that are widely accepted in the West). You should try either of these options on a shorter, local journey before your trip abroad to see if one works for you. You can find Sea-Bands at most drugstores, and Walmart or Target; ginger is easier to find in a supermarket.

Nosebleeds. Travelers who are sensitive to sudden changes in air pressure might resolve themselves to a nosebleed either during or immediately after a long flight. Depending on what kind of environment you live in, you probably won't know how susceptible you are to rupturing a nasal blood vessel until you travel. There are few things that will aggravate your anxiety more than blood running down your face in front of people (and not finding enough tissues in the airplane lavatory), so before your flight, try using a Q-Tip to insert a small amount of ointment (such as Neosporin) into your nostrils. This will greatly reduce the risk of a nosebleed by keeping your sinuses lubricated against the low-humidity air in the plane.

Managing Medication Doses Among Time Zones

On a flight to Switzerland once, I sat next to an elderly woman who wrapped her watch around her three pill bottles, then wondered out loud how she was going to remember to take her medications on Tuesday if it was already going to be Wednesday when we arrived in Zurich. She should have taken a look at the in-flight duty-free catalog, because toward the back was an ad for a pretty decent electronic pillbox. A man across the aisle did in fact buy one during the flight, and we all got to hear how loud an alarm $49.95 buys, and see how organized you can stay by having six little compartments for pills instead of one.

In all seriousness, electronic pillboxes can be very useful if you take two or more medications twice or more per day, and don't want to deal with the math of dosing regimens and time zones. Of course, your doctor can always help you work out such a regimen, as long as you give him or her enough notice before you leave (you still might want to use an alarm, such as on your cell phone, to pull you away from the various travel distractions that threaten your dosing routine).

If you only take one medication, once or twice a day, you might not find an electronic pillbox or dosing regimen adjustment necessary. You may consider taking your medication according to your "old" time zone until you've had a couple days to stabilize at your destination (including getting over travel fatigue) and then start taking it according to your "new" time zone. The most you're going to be early or late in dosing is twelve hours. If you're uneasy about doing this, ask your doctor if it will have a significant impact on your mental health, and the two of you might work out a smoother transition on paper.

How Travel Fatigue Impacts Anxiety

Travel fatigue results from a significant disruption in routine, a low-oxygen environment, and time spent in an isolated, cramped space – namely, all the things that characterize a long-distance flight. Travel fatigue, like fatigue in general, is different from drowsiness or sleepiness; instead of feeling ready to rest, your mind, body, or emotions are still reeling, and you feel too disjointed to do anything but simply lie down. Even though you want nothing more than to sleep, your body won't let you.

Unlike jet lag, travel fatigue can occur without crossing time zones (think, for example, a flight from The Netherlands to South Africa) but since many of us travel long distances either west or east, you will usually have to deal with travel fatigue on top of jet lag. Specific symptoms of travel fatigue include:

- Disorientation and wooziness;
- Decreased level of consciousness and attention;
- Headache; and
- Inability to process stimuli.

While jet lag can linger for a couple of weeks, travel fatigue is far more acute. When within a half-day of traveling people complain of jet lag, what they're usually feeling is travel fatigue. Fortunately, it usually disappears within twenty-four to thirty-six hours, including a night of high-quality sleep.

Some of the effects of travel fatigue are inevitable, but there are ways of strategizing your trip to minimize the stress and anxiety that it causes. A lot has to do with what time you land at your destination. If you arrive in the morning, you could spend all day struggling with the symptoms; if you arrive in the late evening, you could be very restless all night and exhausted the next day. If you arrive in the late afternoon or early evening, however, you give yourself several hours to decompress before a decent night's rest, and can often sleep off the worst of the symptoms.

LAYOVER

Another way to combat travel fatigue is to schedule one or more layovers. Layovers have their disadvantages – in particular, aggravating fear of flying, and often worsening jet lag – but they may be more appealing if you need or want to pace yourself. A good option you may not be aware of is a layover of 20 to 23 hours (a day, essentially), often in a major transit hub such as London or Paris. These are increasingly available as airlines cut down on the frequency of flights, and tweak the timing of their connecting flights; some flights will just miss connecting with each other, and the passenger is offered for sale the next flight on the following day. Many people (particularly business travelers) see this as a big inconvenience, but people on a more leisurely schedule see it as a great chance to see another city for a day. Anxiety sufferers may see it as both that, and a good way to offset travel fatigue.

Here are some other recommendations for managing travel fatigue.

Ask for help. As soon as you land in a foreign environment, you can make as many observations and assessments in a single hour as you would in a day at home. You can boggle your mind with details about who to trust, who to tip, and where to go – all while in a compromised mental and physical state. If your travel companion is a more experienced traveler than you are, forget for a while that you might have something to prove about your independence, and follow their lead. If you're traveling alone, head to the nearest airport information desk, tell them what you need, and let them help you. You've indirectly paid for their services by purchasing your airline ticket.

Postpone driving. Since travel fatigue affects your level of consciousness (including your perceptual abilities) you should be cautious about performing tasks that require constant concentration, such as driving. Driving home from the airport at night after a ten-hour flight – or worse, driving a rental car (day *or* night) in another country right after you've landed – may be setting yourself up for an accident. Abroad, you might consider taking an airport shuttle to an airport hotel, staying one night, and then picking up your rental car to drive wherever you're going. At home, try to pick a landing time that allows you to drive home in daylight, or ask a friend to meet you at the airport and drive you home.

Keep on top of your schedule. Your sense of time, and the amount of time passed, are often compromised when you're suffering from travel fatigue. Not only can you wake up at your first hotel unsure if that faint light outside is dawn or dusk, but you may be convinced that you've spent more than an hour on a tour bus, only to verify that just twenty-five minutes have passed.

If you have a lot of things you need to do on your first day abroad, try jotting them down in sequential order, and think in terms of hours or minutes between activities rather than scheduled times.

How Climate Impacts Anxiety

Vacationing in a different climate than you're used to is often part of the appeal of travel. For many people this means choosing a warm climate; for others, a cold or cool place is different, and – usually by association – exotic. Because people are affected by their environment, and climate is a big part of that environment, a vastly different climate can present unexpected factors that impact your anxiety.

A second consideration is the impact on your physical and mental health of suddenly going from one climate to another. Temperature acclimatization is discussed further below.

GOING HOT, OR COLD?

The dozen or so major climate zones on earth can be loosely classified as cold (including polar, sub-arctic, and continental), or warm/hot (including desert and semiarid, Mediterranean, and tropical), with temperate (mainly oceanic) climates falling in between. There are many popular destinations in both colder places (think Canada, Scandinavia, and Alaska) and warm or hot places (think the Caribbean, Southeast Asia, and Hawaii). Just comparing mental images of these places should help you realize the impact weather can have on a place, its people, and the way of life. In short, whether it's hot or cold can make us behave very differently.

Here are some simplified, but consistent characteristics of cities, countries, and regions in cold climates that can impact your emotional health.

More reserved. Cold weather usually pushes people off the streets and into their homes or buildings. If they're out waiting for a train or bus, or for a store to open, they're usually too busy trying to stay warm to pursue strangers. Being in a place where people are often bundled up (both literally and figuratively) can be far more comfortable to you, particularly if you suffer from social anxiety.

Quieter. Because people spend more of their lives inside and in smaller places, cold-climate destinations tend to be more peaceful than those where people can live, play, work, fight, rally, shop, drag-race, and do lots of other things outside year-round.

More structured. For practical reasons, people in cold climates grow accustomed to planning their lives around the weather, and this sense of structure tends to spill over into the culture. Because the next day or week could bring high winds, heavy snow, or a small variety of weather surprises, arrangements usually aren't made or canceled at the last minute, and contingencies are built into services to avoid people getting stranded or inconvenienced. Being able to count on services and systems can be very reassuring for anxiety sufferers.

Feelings of safety. Stormy and violent weather often triggers an instinctive, collective need for survival that many people find comforting, despite any inconveniences. Most cold-weather societies have lower crime rates than warm-weather societies, and studies have shown lower levels of aggression in these populations (perhaps for physiological reasons, since blood vessels shrink and the body produces different hormones in cold weather).

Depressing. If you already live in a cold climate, then going to a frozen wonderland – no matter how beautiful or interesting it is – could be the last thing you want because you'd like to get away from all that quiet, introverted predictability. Depending on how much you're affected by climate, a place that feels and looks like home could remind you of everything from your job to your ice-damaged car windshield to your broken snow shovel. Choose elsewhere – or go to your northern destination during the few months of the year when it's warmer.

Here are some broad characteristics of warm or hot climates, and how they can impact stress levels.

More stimulation. In general, more sunlight means more energy and more activity. If you've gone from a cold, overcast climate to a tropical paradise, your body will produce significantly more hormones and you could suffer a major case of spring fever – even if it's October or November.

While most people associate a little excitement with a good time, you should consider how your anxiety (including any inherent restlessness or sleeplessness) is affected by overstimulation.

Externalized. Heat relaxes people and often causes them to shed inhibitions; they grow more in touch with their surroundings, and each other. Having fewer boundaries, per se, between yourself and strangers can be stressful – and if you are self-conscious about your body, get used to awkwardness from showing more skin just to avoid dehydration and sun stroke.

Louder. There's usually no storm on the way to stop anyone from bringing the activity outdoors, so expect a warm place to come with more noise. Those fewer inhibitions mentioned above also mean more shouting, arguing, honking, blaring music, outdoor parties, parades, festivals, and impromptu sporting events. Closing the windows of your hotel room usually won't be enough to block it all out.

More unpredictable. No one has to adjust their day or week in order to avoid black ice on a road or a coming blizzard, so people take for granted that they can change plans – including yours. Hotel staff know that the sun will be shining just the same whether your airport shuttle is two hours late or not, and that if they want to close down their breakfast service an hour early, you can saunter out into the perfect morning breeze and find something to eat down the street. Needless to say, the laissez-faire attitudes that you may like at first can quickly become unnerving.

Some of these aggravations can be mitigated by taking your trip in the middle of winter; you will usually get warm, not hot, weather, and the longer nights tend to tone down the chaotic atmosphere. Be aware that many other people have the same idea, so you can often expect more crowds and higher costs.

TEMPERATURE ACCLIMATIZATION

Acclimatization is a physical adjustment to an environmental change. Temperature acclimatization is an inevitable part of transitioning from a cold place to a hot place or vice versa, and can be its own source of anxiety unless you know what to expect, and take steps to minimize the shock to your body.

Lack of acclimatization from a cold climate to a hot climate can be responsible for:

- Lack of energy and general lethargy;
- Increased irritability and aggressiveness;
- Lightheadedness and blackouts;
- Difficulty breathing or a sense of suffocation (particularly if transitioning to a humid environment); and
- Moderate to severe headache, dizziness, or shakiness caused by dehydration.

Lack of acclimatization from a hot climate to a cold climate can be responsible for:

- Sleep disorders;
- Muscle spasms;
- Oversensitivity or overreaction to pain; and
- Heart and circulation irregularities.

In the average acclimatization scenario, you'll experience two significant temperature changes: leaving your cold climate to go to a warm or hot climate, and then returning; or vice versa if traveling to a cold climate. However, there are times when you'll experience more than two shifts. On a South America-Antarctic cruise once, I met some Canadians who left their 20-degree February to arrive in the middle of summer in Argentina (90 degrees and humid) for a few days, only for the temperature to gradually plunge into the 30s and 20s as we sailed into Antarctica. When the ship sailed back up the coast of Argentina, the temperature rose all the way back up to 85 degrees; then, my shipmates had to fly back home where daytime highs had just reached the low 30s.

These travelers went through four major temperature changes in less than three weeks, and had to acclimate each time. By the end of their trip they weren't exhausted; they'd been on such a cruise before, and knew how to adjust. You can smoothly adjust to a hot or cold climate, and offset anxiety caused by sudden temperature shock, by:

1. Drinking hot fluids in hot climates, and cold fluids in cold climates;

2. Taking up moderate exercise in your new environment (i.e., an hour of cycling or power walking per day);

3. Dressing in layers of breathable clothing; and perhaps most importantly,

4. Not overreacting to the new climate (e.g., sitting in the nearest sauna for two hours to "recover" from the cold, or sitting on the air conditioning unit all evening after a hot afternoon).

You can access the climate guides of destinations all over the world at http://www.weather2travel.com/climate-guides/.

How Altitude Impacts Anxiety

For many people, the mountains inspire thoughts of relaxation, perspective, and peace and quiet. Particularly to those who fear or dislike cities, crowded beaches, and long stretches of monotonous highway, the mountains can seem like a default tourist destination – a chance to quite literally "run for the hills." Unfortunately, the effects of high altitude were never mentioned in any of the fairytale-like scenes from the *Sound of Music*, and many people who live at or near sea level may find themselves gasping with surprise upon arriving among the peaks – and not for the right reasons.

Since the air is thinner at high elevation, you take in less oxygen with each breath. This can have several impacts on your body, including decreased appetite, insomnia, dehydration, headache, swelling of hands or feet, and difficulty breathing. Fortunately, many symptoms go away after a few days, and your anxiety should subside as well once you understand how your body reacts.

Extreme altitude is a different story. Once you arrive at or climb to elevations of about 14,000 feet, you are prone to acute mountain sickness, or AMS. Typical symptoms of AMS (which affects about half of all people, rather unpredictably so) include dizziness, nausea, prolonged shortness of breath, migraines, dehydration, fatigue, vomiting, agitation, and light-headedness. The symptoms are often enough to deter or slow even the most well-conditioned mountain hikers or climbers. If you've been considering a "nature trip" at very high elevations, you should think seriously about your ability to manage the potential health effects of AMS. People with anxiety disorders tend to be more naturally sensitive to their environments, and may experience some symptoms well below 14,000 feet.

If you want to try a trip at high elevation despite the risks, don't increase elevation more than a thousand feet per day. If AMS symptoms occur, descend to below where you first felt sick, then re-acclimate to that elevation before taking on a slower-paced climb (or ride). Milder symptoms will resolve themselves in two to three days.

How Topography Impacts Anxiety

Topography refers to the variations in a place's elevation. Places with a varied topography include hilly or mountainous cities next to a lake or ocean; areas with no variation in topography are very flat. A place's topography is a definite factor in its appeal to visitors. Some of the most idyllic and popular cities in the world, such as Vancouver and San Francisco, have a varied topography, with lots of vistas and dramatic backdrops. Such cities can greatly appeal to those with anxiety for psychological reasons you may not be fully aware of.

Consider the following about hilly or mountainous cities.

Easier navigation. You can usually find the horizon, and you have a lot of reference points around you. It's a lot harder to get lost when you can see your hotel a half-mile down a hill.

Sense of security. Many people experience a feeling of enclosure and safety in mountainous or hilly areas, with the landscape providing the semblance of a natural barrier and defense.

More privacy. Particularly if you're up a steep hill, you may feel you have more personal space, without the unwelcome sense of claustrophobia.

Think about how hilly and mountainous cities, both large and small, differ in perception from some of the world's flattest mega-cities such as London, Paris, Tokyo, Los Angeles, New York, and Madrid. Does a sense of confinement and chaos come to mind when you think of the latter places? A lot will depend on your personality, and your experience with cities. Some people will experience flatness as a great sense of expansiveness, with the accompanying feeling of freedom; others — and particularly anxiety sufferers — may feel overwhelmed, disoriented, and distressed by the sprawl that seemingly leads to both everywhere and nowhere. Some very flat cities, including Paris and London, overcome this quality with visually appealing and easily identifiable landmarks set on a relatively low skyline; other cities don't even try.

You can't change a city, but recognizing and addressing any sensitivity you have to an urban environment can go a long way towards managing anxiety. There are reasons that suburbs twenty, and even thirty miles out from mega-cities have so many hotels; you might find one of them to be a nice compromise when traveling to "the flatlands."

Unanticipated Physical Contributors to Anxiety and Panic Attacks While Traveling

Even after you've rested and recovered from travel fatigue, and are successfully managing jet lag, you need to be aware of several physiological problems you may not normally think about that can significantly aggravate your anxiety.

Dehydration. Your body needs fluids just to absorb medication, and any over-the-counter pills you take to ease travel problems (such as diarrhea or motion sickness) can contribute to dehydration. You will exacerbate dehydration if, like many travelers, you consume fewer fluids in order to avoid having to find a bathroom. Even moderate dehydration can make you nauseous, dizzy, and shaky, and contribute to an anxiety or panic attack.

To avoid hassle and stress over having to make sudden runs to the bathroom, try staying hydrated by consuming more fruits and vegetables than water, coffee, soft drinks, etc. The water in fruits and vegetables is absorbed much better and more slowly by your body, and fresh produce can ease any stomachache caused by medications.

Vices out of whack. While your body can gradually get used to heavy smoking and high caffeine consumption, a sudden spike in your caffeine or nicotine intake can contribute to a panic or anxiety attack by significantly raising your blood pressure. If you're a smoker, you could knowingly cause this spike by stepping out of an airport after a twelve-hour flight and having three cigarettes in an hour to make up for your deprivation. You could also unwittingly cause a spike by purchasing and smoking an unfamiliar brand of cigarettes that has far more nicotine than you're used to.

Caffeine intake can be even harder to monitor. Unless you've found a familiar chain such as Starbucks abroad, you could order a coffee drink at a local café that gives you much more of a jolt than you can handle, and shifts your nervous system into overdrive with no easy way to come "down" from the high. If you're sensitive to caffeine intake, ask for light coffee, or – if you get a blank stare – dilute your brew with plenty of milk or water. Another alternative is to head to a local supermarket and buy a pre-packaged coffee drink. Nescafe, Starbucks, and other international brands sell packaged (read: predictable) beverages in the milk aisle.

Food allergies. Eating out on vacation is a highlight for many travelers, but constantly consuming unfamiliar food can lead to an unpleasant discovery of a food allergy you didn't even know you had. Equally as unsettling is stumbling across a known allergy when something that looked "safe" on your plate turns out to be your nemesis. Suddenly feeling ill, or breaking out in hives, in a crowded foreign restaurant can be extremely stressful, and the nausea and vomiting that come with many food allergies can seriously aggravate your anxiety.

If you have a lot of food allergies, or one in particular that is severe, don't get caught up in the atmosphere of the restaurant and forget to ask the waiter or waitress what's in the dish you want to order. If language barriers will be an issue, have your HMO translate your food allergy description for you before you leave, and have this document with you when you eat out.

Hay fever. Allergies can contribute to panic attacks since the body sees an allergen as a "threat" and can produce the "fight or flight" response that often leads to (or comes) with an attack. Although hay fever is usually accompanied by sneezing and sniffling, these symptoms aren't always present, and feelings of hyperactivity or rapid heartbeat from a seemingly unknown cause can be stressful. There are many thousands of plants, weeds, flowers, trees, and other flora growing in large swaths across the earth, and a tourist guidebook is unlikely to mention which could cause an allergic reaction for people who have never been exposed to them.

Before you leave, go to the World Allergy Organization website at http://www.worldallergy.org/pollen/index.php?region=all&country=all&infotype=all&language=all and look up what blooms where you're headed. Talk to your doctor about choosing an antihistamine that's broad enough to treat different types of hay fever, and won't affect or aggravate the side effects of your anxiety medications.

71

CHAPTER 4

Mental Health Perceptions Around the World and How They Can Affect You

Unfortunately, anxiety disorders and their effects on people are often misunderstood or negatively construed in cultures and countries around the globe. You have probably become accustomed to having proper mental health care at home and having the support of family, friends, and society in general when it comes to securing treatment, so it may be hard to imagine that even though anxiety is a universally occurring mental health problem, disorders can be significantly misinterpreted or avoided, and manifestations seen as inappropriate or even offensive.

While some of the regions where mental health problems are misunderstood are not places you might vacation anyway, there are many popular countries that have only a basic understanding of panic and anxiety attacks, and may not demonstrate any increased acceptance or accommodation of foreigners with these disorders. Even in advanced countries where the best care and medications are available, social stigma surrounding mental illness can prevent you from locating a doctor, and otherwise confuse or complicate your access to treatment.

Particularly if you are staying more than a couple weeks in a region, you should understand its basic mental health perceptions and trends regarding care and access. Once you land in a particular country, you become temporarily a part of it, and how much you're affected by the views of its people depends on 1) how insulated you are by a tour group or travel companion, and 2) how much consultation, treatment, or emergency access to medications you may need. Although you may not want to think about it, it is better to understand before (rather than after) you leave if the people in your host country think that mental disorders are caused by divine punishment, a misfortune in the family, bad spirits, polluted air, or many other reasons as diverse as the place and culture itself.

Before we get into details about specific cultures, let's look at some global trends.

Disparity in understanding of anxiety disorders. The more widely you travel, the more you'll notice dramatic differences in people's response to, and understanding of, specific disorders. What you view as common knowledge or common sense about human emotions may be heavily influenced by cultural values and interpretations, to the extent that others will have a significantly different understanding than you'd expect. For example, a prevailing belief in a country may be that all PTSD sufferers experience memory loss, or that anxiety is caused by other illnesses such as epilepsy.

Low priority. With so many sanitary health issues affecting developing countries, tackling mental health tends to be seen as a luxury. Many countries in Africa and Asia do not have mental health policies, plans, or programs simply because they cannot afford them. Foreign aid spending remains focused on combating communicable diseases such as HIV, malaria, and tuberculosis, with other health conditions receiving only a fraction of the attention and funding.

Most resources in large cities. About half the countries in the world have no more than one psychiatrist per 100,000 people, and what professional help does exist is located in capital cities and other metropolises. Depending on where you are, you could require a lot of uncomfortable travel and significant delay in receiving treatment – or even finding a staffed pharmacy.

Either "normal" or "insane." In some cultures there is little attempt to recognize any mental states except healthy ("normal") or psychotic ("insane"). The average person will associate the latter with someone who imagines things; engages in unconscious behavior, such as wandering about; talks to one's self; displays abnormal dressing, sleeping or eating behavior; is oblivious to others; and is agitated or aggressive even when left alone. If you exhibit none of these symptoms (and most of us don't!) then people might be genuinely confused as to why you're seeking help.

Loss of autonomy. Even in countries where you find advanced care, you may need to closely monitor your ability to choose treatment and your right to check out of a clinic or hospital. You may find that the less you characterize your disorder as a psychiatric condition, the better. "Care" bordering on human rights violations can be disturbingly common abroad, with patients isolated, stripped of personal belongings, and denied information and access to communication.

It's now time to take a closer look at mental health perceptions by region, and how they can affect you. At the end of this chapter, we'll look at how to factor this information in to choice of travel destination.

The U.S., Canada, Australia, and New Zealand

In many regards the U.S. Canada, Australia, and New Zealand lead the world in mental health treatment, access, and research. The U.S. and Canada are home to many highly respected international psychiatric organizations, and Australia and New Zealand (which are more similar in model and approach to North America than to Europe) contribute significant advancements in understanding and care. Both regions and their institutions have varying degrees of influence around the globe, and you may take the attitudes and treatment you're familiar with for granted until you travel.

In North America, Australia, and New Zealand (as well as a good portion of the Western world), anxiety disorders are classified as a psychological and physiological condition, marked by persistent fear or worry, that interferes with normal functioning. People who are properly treated for an anxiety disorder are deemed able to function in society and able to lead highly productive and meaningful lives. The treatment of anxiety disorders usually consists of psychotherapy (mainly Cognitive Behavioral Therapy) and psychopharmacology (drugs used to treat mental disorders), with an emphasis on personalized recovery and with general acknowledgement that the benefits of pharmaceutical treatment outweigh the side effects.

A broad and liberal societal understanding of anxiety disorders, combined with plentiful resources and access to care, may occasionally be marred by 1) some misunderstanding and stigma, related to perceived unreliability (being a "basket case" or "unable to pull it together") and 2) less access in poorer or rural regions (including those devastated by budget cuts) where those seeking psychiatric care may be triaged through drug or alcohol recovery programs. It's worth taking a look at some other notable trends in order to compare to other regions of the world.

Treatment at mainstream facilities. Anxiety disorders are most often treated through HMOs (usually via a separate department of psychiatry) and not triaged for treatment at specialized psychiatric hospitals and mental health institutions (as is fairly common abroad).

Influence of psychology. Psychotherapy and psychoanalysis, both Western inventions, are rooted in psychological principles that are considered essential to evaluate anxiety disorders (particularly PTSD and social anxiety disorder). These principles are not necessarily applied in other cultures, where different views of the relationship between mental, emotional, and physical realms may exist.

Combination of therapy and medication. Cognitive Behavioral Therapy (CBT) is used to treat a wide variety of disorders, with the premise that modifying thought patterns and behavior will help address symptoms. Such therapy is considered complementary to the use of psychiatric medications. This might be seen as natural, but some cultures will only encourage or accept the use of either therapy, or medications.

Perception influenced by ethnic background. The U.S., Canada, Australia, and New Zealand have sizeable and diverse immigrant populations, and varying degrees of integration (as well as unpredictable areas of ethnic concentration). You should be aware that while facilities might be identical from place to place within a country, perceptions and attitudes toward mental illness might be different depending on local cultural make-up.

Anxiety disorders vs. psychosis. Those suffering from anxiety disorders and mood disorders are very rarely lumped together (either physically or categorically) with those suffering from psychotic disturbances (including individuals who pose a threat to society and to themselves, and lack full awareness of their own actions).

Belief in treatability. We may take for granted the concept that anxiety disorders and other mental illnesses can be successfully treated and managed. In some countries, such disorders are viewed as incurable and even contagious.

Europe

Fortunately, the most popular and visited continent in the world also boasts generally reliable care that should be familiar to North American tourists. The diverse countries and regions of Great Britain, Scandinavia, Ireland, France, Germany, Italy, Spain, Eastern Europe, Southern Europe, and Russia are more or less united by psychiatric beliefs and approaches that originated in Europe in the late nineteenth century. Reflecting well-established traditions of secularism, there is little remaining religious or superstitious influence (which often viewed mental health problems as a result of tempting evil) and little difference in attitudes between Catholic, Protestant, and Orthodox areas within Europe. You may be subject to more archaic views and more difficult access in Southern Europe (including the former Yugoslav countries) as well as the former Soviet countries, but overall, care reflects the relatively high quality of life and a practical approach to successful treatment. Here are some things to keep in mind.

Accommodation. Europeans are more likely than many others around the world to conform to the idea that as an American (or Canadian), you're accustomed to receiving a certain type of treatment or medications. Many attending physicians have studied (or have cohorts) in North America and are familiar with the moderate differences in systems and care. They may be more flexible than you would expect, i.e., present you with more than one treatment option.

Blaming family members. For various far-reaching cultural reasons,

Europeans tend to link anxiety disorders with psychosocial problems within the family (similar to the North American penchant for blaming your mother/father/brother/etc. for all your "issues"). For this reason, an attending physician may ask an unusual number of questions about who you're traveling with, and may even ask to talk to family member(s) with you.

Psychiatric hospitals. Differences in terminology, categorization, and the influences of national health systems mean that you may be accidentally – or intentionally – triaged to a mental health hospital or institution. There is no need to go to a psychiatric hospital since you'll be able to access the resources you need at a general hospital or clinic.

Remember that in countries where national health care services are available, you'll have to pay full prices up front just like you would at a private hospital since you're not a resident of the country.

Relation to unemployment. Like North America, Europe is a consumerist culture; unlike North America, it suffers from staggeringly high unemployment in several areas, particularly among the young and among those nearing retirement age. Be aware that some mental health care access and operating hours may be tied to unemployment benefits or outreach, and steer away.

Psychosomatic and physical manifestations. Because of cultural tendencies to avoid (but not ignore) mental health problems, Europeans may report somatic symptoms such as headaches, stomach pains, and "nerve troubles" instead of admitting anxiety triggers and phobias. Your straightforwardness in describing symptoms, and your existing diagnosis, may be unexpected and appreciated by an attending physician – who will probably out of habit ask about psychosomatic problems you may be having.

Japan and South Korea

These countries (Japan in particular) are popular and modern tourist destinations with state-of-the-art medical facilities and reliable and plentiful pharmacies. One reason that Japan and South Korea interest travelers is because both cultures have many vastly different ways of seeing and doing things than in the West; this section will help you navigate the drawbacks of this aspect when it comes to treatment of anxiety disorders, so you can get back to the best of what both countries have to offer.

Medications-only approach. Unless you've found a Western-style hospital or clinic, you'll notice a heavy emphasis on pharmaceutical treatment. An attending physician is likely to write you a prescription with little acknowledgment of behavioral therapy or management techniques for a disorder. Most psychotherapy treatment is reserved for long-term inpatients only.

Avoidance and embarrassment. Displays of emotion, including those that inevitably come with anxiety or panic attacks, will undoubtedly make surrounding people uncomfortable and uneasy. They may not acknowledge the situation, or will only if 1) your manifestations are perceived as a physical breakdown, or 2) for the sake of assisting you as a foreigner (particularly if you're alone). If you are experiencing severe anxiety, it may be best to stay in your hotel room, and ask for help over the phone.

Underutilized treatment. Although advanced treatment and medications are available for many mental health disorders, government studies repeatedly conclude that many sufferers never seek professional help due to social expectations to overcome a disorder alone (or manage it with the assistance of family). While this may be depressing or upsetting to think about, it also means you should have no trouble finding the care you need, when and how fast you need it.

Lack of willpower. The loss of control over one's mind or physiology (including the nerves) is often seen as an inability to exert willpower, or strength. Perhaps more than in other cultures, men will make less sympathetic subjects than women when seeking treatment for anxiety.

Respect for the different needs of foreigners. As in Europe, people will usually understand and respect that Westerners are accustomed to their own treatment, and try to find you what you're familiar with to make you comfortable. This can go a little overboard, to the extent that you feel isolated or awkward, but accommodating attitudes and efforts can certainly be helpful in getting you the care you need.

China

In many ways China is a country of extremes, with standards, resources, and practices varying dramatically across the country, and psychiatric care is no different. China is also one of the fastest growing tourist destinations in the world, with many travelers planning and taking their own trips despite significant cultural and language barriers.

Hong Kong, which is viewed by many as part of China and by many others as still an independent entity, is very westernized and accessible, including over twenty major hospitals with near-identical care to what you would receive at home, and fluent English-speaking staff. The following considers mainland China.

Inconsistency in standards. Only in the last thirty years or so – with the relaxation of communist attitudes and controls – have western models of psychiatric treatment been introduced in China, and there are a growing number of western hospitals in the large cities (including Beijing, Shanghai, and Tianjin). Access to westernized care in rural areas (particularly in the far west) ranges from challenging to find, to virtually nonexistent.

Human rights concerns. Only in 2012 did China adopt laws protecting the human rights of mental health patients, including a person's right to not be hospitalized against their will, and to choose whether to receive treatment. You'll need to be very careful about what care you consent to, and under what conditions. In more rural areas without western hospitals, it would be best if you did not go to a clinic alone. If you have no travel companion, try asking a hotel employee to come with you, just to be safe.

Financial motives. Unfortunately there have been cases of foreigners being over-treated in hospitals or clinics with the goal of collecting more money for services rendered. While it's highly unlikely you would be given medications of improper dosage, you'll need to be careful to only approve of and receive the amount of care you see fit. While it's true that money is just money, the trauma of being misled and dealing with an exorbitant and unfair bill is not going to do your nerves any good.

Preoccupation with suicide. High suicide rates (often attributed to modernization and pressure to succeed, particularly among young people) is a serious problem in China, particularly in the cities. Despite your status as a tourist, an attending physician may ask you a number of questions related to suicidal tendencies and self-harm.

Limited public tolerance. Be careful about showing any overt psychiatric symptoms in public, particularly near police. Certain elements of a panic or anxiety attack may be viewed as a disturbance of the peace, and you may receive only minimal leniency for being a foreigner.

Southeast Asia

Thailand, Malaysia, Vietnam, and The Philippines are very popular tourist destinations that can be simultaneously welcoming, threatening, relaxing, and bewildering. Many areas are very poor and lack Western facilities or attitudes toward mental illness. The majority of travelers visit these beautiful areas and countries as part of a tour, which can insulate them considerably from the views of the region, as well as provide familiar medical treatment. Here is some information you'll need if you strike out on your own, or with an inexperienced travel companion.

(Indonesia, which is also in the region, will be covered in the subsection on Muslim countries.)

Lack of awareness. While people generally understand that anxiety disorders alter normal functioning and include physical manifestations, many cannot correctly discern them from illnesses such as epilepsy and schizophrenia, and are unaware of the medications used for treatment. You should leave home with the name and directions to a doctor and pharmacy (or better yet, several of each) rather than attempting to locate services once at your destination.

Cerebral and intellectual connection. In many areas of Southeast Asia, mental illness and anxiety disorders are heavily associated with mental overload, i.e., from taking on too much or "over-thinking." The first thing an attending physician may tell you is to rest and relax without necessarily acknowledging a diagnosis or need for medications.

Buddhist influence. Thailand, Laos, Vietnam, Myanmar, and Cambodia are predominantly Buddhist, with spiritual influences having an overall positive impact on attitudes and views of self-understanding, wellness, and overcoming or confronting suffering

84

(including anxiety).

Stress and "nerve problems." The average individual (including hotel clerks and other staff you may encounter) may not distinguish between the terms *anxiety, stress, nerves,* and *depression.* A high percentage of people in the region are forthcoming about discussing stress, readily acknowledging the hectic pace of life amidst expectations to succeed, but the idea that you would need to go to a doctor for "anxiety" may seem bizarre to them.

Family care. As in some other developing parts of the world, family members are expected to care for and speak for the needs of people with mental illness. When you seek treatment, you're likely to be handled differently if you are traveling with a family member than if you are traveling independently or with friends or a group.

India

This great, vast country has an international reputation as a center of personal awareness, spiritual improvement, and well-being, and is at or near the top of many travel wish-lists. Cultural focuses on meditation and the mind-body connection, however, should not be confused with an interest or attempt to address mental illness, including anxiety disorders. The remnants of British influence and the widespread following of Hinduism, which promotes tolerance and understanding, inspire a mix of traditional and modern views of anxiety. Here are some things to be aware of.

Urban and rural divide. Unfortunately, widespread poverty in the countryside mires many attempts to introduce or maintain Western-style hospitals. You may encounter lack of recognition, counterfeit medications, and limited facilities if seeking consultation in rural areas. Many country dwellers believe that fasting, daily worship, or a faith healer can help improve anxiety. If culture shock and widely divergent views cause you significant stress, you should think seriously before venturing outside the major cities either alone or with an inexperienced travel companion.

Perception of incurability. There are widespread beliefs that mental illnesses, including anxiety disorders, are untreatable or self-inflicted, and that while you may improve your condition, you cannot achieve "recovery" per se. You might also encounter fatalistic attitudes and perceptions that you should make yourself as comfortable as possible, and stop "fighting" your disorder.

Shunning of psychiatrists. Despite some improvements in recent years, many people still believe that psychiatrists are eccentric and unproductive, and may not even recognize psychiatry as a branch of medicine. Do not ask for a psychiatrist or psychiatric care when arriving at a medical clinic or facility; ask for a general care practitioner.

Fear of the affected. Many people, particularly outside the cities, believe that aspects of mental illness can be transmitted to others – or at the least, that sufferers are a very negative influence. If you exhibit symptoms outside of a medical facility, you may be subject to reproach or suspicion.

Great range in the belief of causes. You might encounter a preoccupation with the cause of your anxiety disorder, both from an attending physician and from the people who help you locate treatment. Heredity, psychological or emotional shock, marital conflicts, brain disturbance, and the physical environment are all thought to contribute to anxiety disorders, depending on where you are and who you talk to.

Latin America

Despite some regional variations, Latin American countries (including Mexico, Central America, and South America) generally embrace Western models of recognizing and treating psychiatric illness. The richest three countries – Argentina, Uruguay, and Chile – have modeled themselves more after European than North American institutions and systems of care. Countries where indigenous Native American populations still have considerable influence, such as Brazil and Peru, are likely to harbor more superstitions and belief in the role of traditional healers to treat mental illness. In Argentina and Uruguay, where populations are overwhelmingly of European (Spanish and Italian) descent, this influence is almost nonexistent. Here are some other things to keep in mind.

Secularism despite appearances. Church-run hospitals fill many of the social welfare gaps left by under-funded public care systems. Don't hesitate to seek care at a Catholic hospital; in most cases you will receive modern care with no association or expectation of religiosity, or bias if you're not Catholic.

Distorted help-seeking patterns. Somewhat similar to Europeans, Latin Americans are prone to deeply rooted cultural biases to disguise mental health issues as other problems in order to avoid shame and guilt. Doctors have heard any number of rationales for symptoms of anxiety disorders, with sufferers self-diagnosing ulcers, hyperactivity, or fast heartbeat in order to secure tranquilizers and sedatives. An attending physician will appreciate your straightforwardness in describing your established diagnosis and current symptoms.

Emphasis on hospital care. In most areas the preferred place of treatment for mental health problems is the hospital, with high priority placed on psychotherapy and time needed to recover. You might find that your approach of anxiety management in the real world, and moving on with your trip, are met with caution by an attending physician. Understand that concerns are rooted in good intentions and the belief in more formalistic care, and don't be afraid to part ways once you've gotten your consultation and medications.

Domestic violence cases. Unfortunately, reported cases of domestic violence are high in Latin America compared to other regions, and many victims are forthcoming about anxiety caused by abuse. If you are a woman you might be questioned about whether you're a victim of domestic violence or rape.

Empathy and relatively positive attitudes. The general populace of Latin America has significantly more positive attitudes toward mental illness and disorders than many parts of Asia and Africa. You're far more likely to be met with openness and understanding than avoidance and alienation.

The Caribbean

On the whole, Caribbean Islanders tend to have a fairly narrow view of mental illness; the degree to which they apply this view to foreigners can be unpredictable. A widespread belief is that people should sort out their problems (including those related to anxiety) within the family, and not expose personal and private information to strangers. The result is that mental illness is often addressed with the same level of public confidence and directness as sexual dysfunction. Of course, for such a relatively small region, the Caribbean is highly diverse, with beliefs influenced by Latin America (namely, the Catholic Church) and African folk rituals (Voodoo in Haiti, Obeah in Jamaica, and Santeria in Cuba). When you are traveling and uncertain of your ability to manage your anxiety independently, try to stay as close to a vacation resort as possible. If that isn't realistic, here are some things to be aware of.

Assumed connection to substance abuse. Rates of drug addiction are very high in many areas of the Caribbean, and since symptoms of drug withdrawal often resemble those of an anxiety or panic attack, your manifestations may be attributed to drug abuse. Be prepared to answer questions about substance abuse if seeking treatment.

Significant stigma. Many anxiety sufferers don't seek help because mental illness carries a serious stigma and is often lumped under the term "madness." With societal stigma comes difficulty in getting information about psychiatric care, and possibly uncomfortable conversations with an attending physician.

Matter of willpower. Unfortunately, beliefs abound that mental illness, including anxiety disorders, can be controlled by determination and the avoidance of negative or self-defeating thoughts. Men more than women are likely to be met with reproach when acknowledging anxiety or other psychiatric problems.

Aid of clergy. A high percentage of locals may turn to clergy and other spiritual leaders for help with "emotional problems," including anxiety. A well-meaning person (including hotel employees or other staff) could direct you to the local church if you express complications related to anxiety.

Family and social network. Because of limited public funding for health problems, the family and its social ties plays an important role in helping an individual cope with an anxiety disorder. This attitude may be applied to foreigners, with an attending physician expressing undue concern if you are traveling alone.

Sub-Saharan Africa

While not a first-choice destination for the inexperienced traveler, Sub-Saharan Africa (meaning the continent of Africa minus the far northern countries such as Morocco, Libya, Algeria, and Egypt) is popular for safari activities and other wildlife attractions. The country of South Africa also attracts sizeable numbers for its cultural and sporting events. Unfortunately, with the exception of some cities and areas in South Africa, most areas and countries have limited medical resources, no mental health policies, and limited awareness of anxiety disorders. Attitudes and perceptions of mental health problems are influenced by native cultural-religious beliefs; the degree of Westernization affected by the colonizing force; the amount of resources available; and the prevalence of communicable diseases in the region. Here are some other things to understand.

Association of mental disorders with HIV infection. In many African countries, people suffer from acute psychosis due to the cerebral impact of infectious diseases (such as typhoid fever and malaria) and HIV. If you try to explain your mental health condition, or show significant symptoms, a less informed professional may assume a correlation with one of these illnesses.

Priority for those with brain damage. Because of severe malnutrition, neglect, and stunted psychosocial development, brain damage and mental retardation are two of the main sources of mental health treatment in this region. Incidents of brain infection and trauma are also much higher in Sub-Saharan Africa than in other regions of the world. If you're lucky enough to find a medical clinic or pharmacy that can help you, prepare to have your needs and concerns assigned a low priority.

Undiagnosed PTSD. Many countries in Africa are (or were recently) engulfed in conflicts and civil strife, with a significant adverse impact on the mental health and well-being of the affected populations. An unknown percentage of civilians suffer from undiagnosed PTSD. Unfortunately, PTSD is often not recognized as a disorder at all, but viewed as "dealing with life." If you exhibit symptoms resembling PTSD, it may be hard to get recognition from anyone but a physician, and you may be mistaken for someone traveling from a nearby troubled area instead of a tourist.

Short-handedness. While in Europe there about 400,000 psychiatrists and specialists for a population of 840 million, in Africa there are about 14,000 psychiatrists and specialists for about 620 million people. Although I've emphasized that a general care practitioner will usually prove the most useful to you, bear in mind the limited resources in this region, and consider accepting help from whoever recognizes the medications and condition you are talking about.

Counterfeit medications. These are rampant, since what African authorities do exist are busy fighting the illegal drug trade. We'll talk more about how to identify counterfeit medications in Chapter 8.

Domination of traditional healers. These individuals are prevalent in both the cities and the countryside, and have a good reputation for helping people. Unfortunately, many of them (who may very well be called "doctors") are strongly against any medication intake, so a well-meaning person who has steered you in the direction of a healer will complicate your mission to find a pharmacy, if one exists.

The Middle East, North Africa, and Indonesia (The Muslim World)

Perhaps more than any other region, attitudes toward mental health problems in the Middle East, North Africa, and Indonesia are influenced by religious beliefs. Islam generally views mental illness as a result of an unbalanced body or lifestyle. Mental illness is regarded as a disorder (not a disease) that affects a person's cognitive, social, emotional, and behavioral state; people with mental illness are usually received with understanding and tolerance. It's likely that some of the first psychiatric hospitals in the world were built in the Middle East (Cairo and Baghdad), and the region continues to contribute research and pharmaceutical developments in the treatment of anxiety disorders. Here are some trends you may observe while seeking care.

Variety of causes. Given the belief in a wide range of causes for anxiety, an attending physician may inquire about your diet, sleep patterns, heredity, stress level, brain accident or injury, or even drug use. Be patient with these questions and understand that they are a means to an end.

Broad treatment. Anxiety disorders are medically defined and treated using psychiatric models similar to those in the West. You should be aware, however, that given a more integrated and God-centric world view in the region, doctors may regard traditional medicine, folk healers, and pharmaceutical treatment as complementary in nature. Upon seeking treatment, you may be offered more than just a consultation and a prescription; no one will be offended if you politely decline.

Private support. Unfortunately, government funding for the treatment of mental illness is not viewed as a priority in many countries of the region, so public institutions or access can be lacking. You're more likely to find advanced and appropriate care at a private institution – particularly a university-run facility.

Urban and rural divide. Attitudes and approaches to treatment are likely to be far more predictable in the city than in rural areas. It is important to note that supernatural causes of illness are still widely acknowledged within Islam – predominantly in the countryside.

No association with religious practice. Mental illness is not believed to correlate to religion, or lack of religious belief. In other words, the chance of someone attributing your anxiety disorder to being a non-Muslim is slim to none. In a part of the world where religion is a sensitive topic, you might find this reassuring.

How Cultural Perceptions of Mental Illness, and Availability of Mental Health Resources, Factor Into Your Choice of Destination

After reading this chapter, you may think that you shouldn't visit one of the poorer developing countries since they pose too many barriers and risks to your psychiatric health. However, you should consider why you wanted to visit such a country in the first place. Developing countries often lack the subtle but chronic stressors that you may be trying to escape from. They can be exhilaratingly lax and fun, pulling you out of your head and into the moment, and making you wonder what you were even worried about when you left home. Although you should always have a plan to manage an anxiety or panic attack abroad, the sub-par standards of medical facilities won't be much of a factor if you're too relaxed to have a care in the world.

You should understand how you feel about the importance of safety, access, and cultural factors when making your final decision and booking a ticket to a place that you've wanted to see for years. If you're nervous about going to a place that isn't ideal to host someone with an anxiety disorder, consider waiting until after you have more travel experience at "safer" destinations, or go with a large tour that has its own doctor and access to medical facilities. Or, choose to stay at a large Western chain hotel in a city center where you will be more insulated from unfamiliar medical practices and attitudes. The next chapter includes information on hotels with in-house physicians.

In Chapter 8 we'll talk about how to overcome cultural barriers to get help during a psychiatric emergency, but for now, consider the following questions.

Are the mental health attitudes of the region you want to visit going to have a significant impact on your travel plans? How?

_____

_____

What challenges are you willing to accept (such as significant language barrier, potential embarrassment and stigmatization, long distances to travel for treatment, etc.) by traveling to a country where access to a psychiatrist or medications is challenging?

_____

_____

_____

What challenges are you *unwilling* to accept?

_____

_____

_____

Will this influence your overall decision of where to travel? How?

_____

_____

_____

The Anxious Person's Guide to
Planning a Trip

Now that you have a better personal understanding of the world, yourself as a traveler, and your anxiety, we'll look at how to transform your trip from daydream to reality. This chapter goes over the all-important pros and cons of different types of lodging, including how to tailor your choice to your specific concerns and anxiety triggers. We'll explore how far you feel comfortable traveling, when you should and shouldn't travel, and how to plan an itinerary that you'll find stimulating but not overwhelming. You'll recognize the benefits and drawbacks of touring with a Professional Travel Companion, and the challenges of traveling in rural areas or taking an adventure trip. We'll also go into detail on the mundane but important matters of locating psychiatric care abroad, preparing your emergency contact card, and choosing the proper travel insurance and medevac insurance. By the end of this chapter you'll feel ready and confident to go on a major trip abroad.

How Far to Go

If you've been thousands of miles away from home before and suffered minimal anxiety over the distance between yourself and the places, people, and things that define you, then you have one less travel hurdle to overcome. Others, however, find little comfort in the old traveler's saying *Wherever you go, there you are.* You may suffer from disorientation, a sense of being stranded, or feel as if you're not even under the same sun and same sky on another continent. Understanding your comfort level with distance will help you determine how far you can go and still enjoy your trip.

Of course, your ease with being away can depend on who you're traveling with, how safe you feel in your destination country – and how direct your travel route is. For example, if you live in San Francisco and take a direct flight to London, you might not feel as far away from home than if you needed three flights, a bus drive, and a ferry to reach your destination. Here are some other factors to consider in assessing how far to go.

Similar environment. To make yourself more comfortable, you might pick a place that (at least on the surface) reminds you of home. For example, if you live in soggy but beautiful Portland, Oregon and go to soggy but beautiful Dublin, Ireland, you might think you've landed in a parallel universe. However, if you take a trip from Oregon to Arizona, you could feel like you've fallen off the face of the known world and into the deserts of Sub-Saharan Africa, with the ensuing feelings of discombobulation and distress. A lot depends on how sensitive you are to your natural environment.

Traveling with people you know. If you voyage overseas with your entire immediate family, you may feel like you haven't gone far at all. This can be reassuring or not, depending on how you feel about your loved ones.

Physical versus emotional distance. It sometimes helps to think of being so many hours away from home rather than number of miles away. For example, if you've taken a direct flight from New York to Moscow, you're "only" ten hours away from everything you're familiar with, rather than an insurmountable-sounding 4,600 miles.

Emotional distance can often be measured in culture shock. If you travel from Venice, California to Venice, Italy you might not notice the 6,100 mile difference between the two cities. Traveling 1,875 miles from Minnesota to Cuba might result in a different feeling altogether.

Is it really about you? If you're traveling thousands of miles alone, or only with a Professional Travel Companion, it may be hard for your loved ones to avoid worrying about what you'll do if you have an anxiety or panic attack. A lot of *their* anxiety arises from being unable to visualize where you'll be staying and what you'll be seeing and doing (in contrast, you have a pretty good mental image of what they'll be doing while you're gone). Staying on the same continent on your first major trip may ease the stress on both sides. This also gives you a chance to establish a phone call, email, or Skype travel routine with the people most concerned about you.

When to Go

For people who don't have an anxiety disorder, "when to go" usually boils down to when they have enough time and money saved up to travel, and what season offers the best weather at their destination. For us, "when to go" depends far more on our current mental and emotional health. We need more strategizing, personal evaluation, and knowledge in order to ready ourselves for the challenge and excitement of travel. If you need several months after reading this book to absorb all the information and approach travel as an activity rather than a goal, that's fine. But if you try to take on too much of the world too fast, you could backlash against traveling and be afraid to try again for months or even years.

Here are some guidelines for identifying your readiness to take a trip in the near future.

Stability in medications. It's generally unwise to travel just after switching from one anti-anxiety medication to another, or significantly changing doses. Even medications in the same class of drugs can affect you quite differently. Almost all medications require a considerable adjustment period, with moderate or significant side effects decreasing over time.

A new medication can change how you react to different stimuli, and may affect your stamina and tolerance. If you've started taking something new, don't go on a major trip until you know what to expect of yourself and the impact of fatigue, adrenaline, and other physical factors on your system. Of course, this is something you should discuss with your psychiatrist.

Stability in treatment. If your doctor just started you on a new cognitive behavioral therapy program such as visualization techniques, you may want to wait until you're accustomed to doing them (and have some success with them) before you go away. Not only will there be travel-induced disruptions such as long plane rides to challenge your therapy routine, but you might find that you can't practice the new technique in a completely different and distracting setting. Again, this is something you can talk more to your psychiatrist about.

Life-changing events. Traveling just after a death in the family, an illness, or significant personal or professional changes (including positive ones, such as the birth of a grandchild or a major promotion at work) could prove overwhelming and exhausting. You may find yourself constantly thinking about home, and make potentially dangerous mistakes in your travel environment under the weight of your distractions. Your mind and heart will greatly appreciate time to process one major development in your life before you move on to the next one.

Anticipation and acknowledgment. If, after reading this book, you still can't name the specific travel factors that will or may increase your anxiety, you might not be prepared to take a major trip. You should think more about what's making you nervous, and talk to your psychiatrist and the people you trust about your misgivings. Try taking day trips that will externalize your phobias, or going to www.theanxioustraveler.com to see what other travelers with anxiety disorders have to share about their uncertainties and how they're addressing them.

How Long to Go, and How Long to Spend in One Place

One of the reasons people decide not to join a travel tour is that they feel the tour is either too short or too long, or that the tour will cover too much ground and they'll feel rushed – or will move along too slowly for them. Anxious people are prone to both restlessness and to feeling overwhelmed easily, so thinking about both the pacing and length of a trip is essential. Your personality, age, and the conditions at your destination also factor in to how fast you wish to tour, and how long you vacation for.

Good travel guidebooks offer suggestions on how much time to allow to explore a certain place. They make these estimates based on the time the average person needs in order to feel neither rushed nor bored. This isn't much different for people with anxiety disorders, except that you should build enough contingency time into your schedule to 1) allow for a morning or evening here or there when you don't feel up to going out, and 2) provide you with a second chance at a sightseeing interest where original plans went awry (such as a museum that was closed on the day you first tried to go) so that you don't feel upset about missing something.

If you feel confident that you can handle a more compressed sightseeing schedule, here are some factors to consider.

Easier to move on. If you spend only a couple days at each place on your itinerary, you're less likely to have a difficult time saying good-bye to each one. You may pass through too quickly to suffer culture shock; rather, if you're passing from country to country in a region, you may experience a more subtle and more manageable "fish out of water" syndrome (I've had it, and it's not bad). You also don't have the time and opportunity to establish a routine in one place, only to break it after a week or so. Because you never get used to anything, you stay more in the moment instead of falling into a rut.

102

Getting overwhelmed. The more you move around, the higher your risk of getting lost, delayed, or losing baggage or other belongings. If you have booked a "circuit trip" of one-way travel and you fall behind, you can find out how quickly your plans can crumble. As an example, I booked six one-way flights around Europe in April 2010 when an Icelandic volcano suddenly erupted and forced me to improvise as regional air traffic to a screeching halt. I got delayed by seven hours at one airport, had to sleep overnight at another, was diverted from Norway to Sweden a couple days later, and entirely missed the second-to-last flight. While I eventually saw what I wanted to see, and I enjoyed myself, some people would liken my experience to navigating an obstacle course rather than taking a vacation.

A more "successful" trip. For a variety of reasons, many people with anxiety disorders can view a tour of a city or country as a goal – something to achieve. For example, when I travel, I want to cover as much ground as possible, partly because I want to experience as many great cultural monuments as I can with the time and money I have, and partly because I just love the feel of moving. You should always step back and ask yourself if you're enjoying your trip, or if you feel weighed down by your own expectations.

Europe, in particular, is ideal for people who eagerly want to experience and check off their list as many things as possible. Doing so isn't unusual or reckless. Think about why Eurail train passes are so popular – you generally pay the same amount whether you take five major train journeys in seven days, or one. Countries are very close together, tempting you to drift from one cultural gem to another until you've passed through three countries in a single week. There's nothing wrong with this, as long as it's what you want and it doesn't aggravate your anxiety disorder.

If you feel tired just reading any of the above, then build yourself a slower-paced vacation.

How Long to Go?

For a trip to another continent, anything less than seven days is really not enough to justify the time on the plane or all the planning involved. You may rule out three- to four-week trips until you've had some experience traveling. A ten- to fourteen-day trip may be ideal to start with since it 1) makes the long hours of travel worth your while, 2) allows you a day or two breather in the middle of the trip, and 3) still gives you plenty of days to see a lot of great things before you start getting tired.

Sequencing your Itinerary

If you're not going to be part of a tour, you should think about the order in which you see attractions and cities, as well as how to best schedule train, bus, ferry rides, and the like to give yourself time to sit and decompress. Common sense can guide you here, since many of us understand the need for a slower day or two in between several hectic days. You can also learn a lot about how to sequence an itinerary by looking up and studying standard tours on the internet.

Beyond all this, there's likely to be one part of your trip that you're most nervous about, that requires particular consideration when it comes to scheduling. This could be:

- A very tight connection: you play over and over in your head missing your connecting flight, or train

- Significant culture shock, such as journeying from Spain into Morocco and back, or Australia to Indonesia

- Uncertainty about the safety or conditions at a hotel, attraction, or area

- A physical challenge, such as having to walk from a small village to a national park because there is no taxi or bus service

... or many others. My best suggestion is to schedule the portion of your trip that you're most worried about in the *middle* of your vacation time. This gives you time to "warm up" as a traveler (preferably in a place where there are relatively few challenges, such as a smaller English-speaking city) so that by the middle of your trip you're in a good travel groove, but still have quite a lot of energy left. Remember, the part you're most nervous about may lead to the part of your trip that you're most excited about, so you don't want to have the attitude of "getting it all over with." You don't want to save it for last either, since you might spend a significant portion of the trip preoccupied with it.

Finishing on a "high note." Say you want to take a trip to Austria and Germany in the fall. Most of your schedule is fixed around visits to Vienna and Innsbruck, a boat trip on a small lake, and visiting a couple of castles in Bavaria, but you have some flexibility regarding which of two places you visit last: the Dachau Nazi concentration camp, where your grandparents died, and the Oktoberfest beer festival in Munich (the two sites are within 15 miles of each other). Even if you find it symbolic to visit the camp memorial last, think about how you would be affected by going from a major festival to one of the most emotionally draining places in Europe. Would you go a little out of your way to book the Dachau visit, and *then* the Oktoberfest?

Variety versus burnout. When sequencing your itinerary, you should consider your physical, mental, and emotional stamina, and the natural human need to alternate activities. Have you scheduled trips to five museums in two days, after three days in a row at the beach?

Do you have four days in a row where you sit on a bus, followed by four days of heavy walking? Does your trip have a definable *beginning, middle,* and *end,* or is it possible you might exhaust yourself the first few days and spend the rest of the trip getting over exhaustion, blistered feet, or emotional overload?

Imagine that you've booked a trip to Barcelona, Spain. Try putting in order the following activities according to what's most comfortable and natural to you.

Sitting on the beach
Going shopping
Taking the train to Madrid and back
Trying karaoke at a local bar
Photographing all the major sites
Watching a bullfight
Snorkeling in the Mediterranean
Lying in your room and just relaxing

Day 1 _____

Day 2 _____

Days 3-4 _____

Day 5 _____

Day 6 _____

Days 7-8 _____

Days 9-10 _____

Day 11 _____

Write your own proposed trip activities here, and try putting them in the most comfortable order:

Day 1 _____

Day 2 _____

Days 3-4 _____

Day 5 _____

Day 6 _____

Days 7-8 _____

Days 9-10 _____

Day 11 _____

What to Plan and What to Leave Up in the Air

There's a fine line between sequencing your itinerary to make yourself comfortable, and pinning every activity to a specific time each day. If you work out every small detail of your daily itinerary, you could feel burdened and restricted; the pressure of sticking to a fixed schedule is often unnecessary, and its own source of stress. Planning ahead, and booking ahead, usually provides you with guarantees that will reduce your anxiety about traveling, and is easier than ever thanks to electronic booking and pre-pay services; however, you can take this overboard. I know of people who've made dinner reservations at three-star restaurants before they've even left the country; I've also met people who landed in a foreign country with no return ticket purchased and not a single hotel reservation made. It's wise to find a happy medium between these two extremes.

It helps to understand the rationales of both the "over-planners" and the "under-planners." The "over-planners" didn't want to be bothered with making decisions, large or small, on their trip; they certainly didn't want to worry about finding a back-up restaurant if their original plans didn't work out. The "under-planners" didn't want to make hotel reservations until they personally saw their choice of hotels in a certain area, and because they were unsure if they'd be in a particular city, province, or even country on a certain day. To them there was an enormous amount of stress in ensuring that they were on the doorstep of *x* hotel at *y* time in *z* city, instead of just "going with the flow." And once they stopped having a good time on their impromptu tour, they simply showed up at the airport and bought their tickets home.

It's not recommended for you to leave for a foreign country without a return ticket home, and it may be pushing your tolerance for stress to not book accommodations ahead of time. An exception to not booking lodging ahead of time may be in rural areas during the off-season, in an area you're familiar with, where there are plenty of hotels to pick from.

As far as secondary transportation goes, you can now buy train tickets, bus tickets, ferry tickets, and even make taxi reservations online well in advance. Whether you choose to do so will depend on 1) the demand for such services; 2) whether reservations can be changed or are refundable; 3) your confidence in being able to be at the right stop or street at the right time; and 4) whether advanced booking will cause you to fixate on times and dates, and drain the energy out of your trip. The same applies to advance purchase of event tickets such as movie showings, zoo admission, and the like.

Assess your own preferences and tolerance level for traveling more spontaneously.

What were you considering booking in advance, that you now think you'll handle when you arrive?

_____

_____

_____

How about vice versa?

_____

_____

_____

Do you feel a sense of freedom or a sense of fear by not working out the fine details of your itinerary ahead of time?

_____

_____

_____

Do you think you could ease your anxiety by living more spur-of-the-moment? If not, why not?

_____

Choice of Transportation

In general, planes take us long distances and over oceans, while trains, cars, and ships fill in the shorter distances. In many cases you won't have much of a choice about the type of transportation you take: for example, if you want to explore the national parks of Europe, renting a vehicle is essential; if you want to go to Antarctica (and unless you're a research scientist or a millionaire with a private plane) ship may be the only practical way to make it there. However, in many cases you may have to decide whether to travel by:

Car or plane (mainly in North America, Australia, and other places without much rail infrastructure); or

Train or plane (mainly in Europe, or across countries such as Japan or New Zealand).

Just as people in the U.S. debate whether to drive or fly from San Francisco to San Diego, or from New York to Washington, D.C., people in Europe debate whether to fly or take the train from Paris to Madrid, or Rome to Munich. This section focuses on weighing the anxiety impacts of planes versus trains. We'll talk more in Chapter 7 about the particular challenges of traveling by rental car and by ship.

TRAINS VS. PLANES

The unpredictability of airport facilities. In a world where international chains, stores, and facilities replicate themselves thousands of times over on the face of the earth, it may come as a surprise that no two commercial airports are truly identical. They can differ by how travelers get around them; by the number of terminals; by how domestic and international flights are segregated;

by customs triage processes; by the breadth and scope of amenities available; and many other factors. There may or may not be a train, shuttle, metro, or bus transfer service to and from the city center. Some large airports have no commuter links to their cities except by taxi; others expect you to take a train, and then a bus, and then another train just to get from the first terminal to the fourth of fifth terminal. Airports are truly a product of their metropolitan environment, influenced by building codes, the amount of space available, and the culture of their state, province or country.

Statistically speaking, airports tend to undergo more frequent renovations (and impose the accompanying detours) than train stations, which can add to the chaos and stress. Another complication involves getting back to the airport from a large foreign city; you often have to worry about using the shuttle or transit to the *correct* airport, since many metropolitan areas have both domestic and international airports.

Getting used to trains. Since taking the train (not just the metro) isn't a part of daily life in North America, you may feel intimidated about booking one overseas. Once you get to understand them, though, trains and train stations are much more straightforward than airports, and may present a lot less stress. Almost every train station on a tourist's path has a main entry hall, ticket counters, some shops and stalls, and anywhere from two tracks to three dozen tracks. The trains themselves are easy to board once you get used to looking for car numbers, seat numbers, and first versus second class cars. Almost all train stations have connecting buses and/or taxis waiting outside. No (or very minimal) security checks means one less layer of complexity. Finally, you get to keep your belongings with you, encounter fewer lines, and generally feel more in control of yourself.

The obvious question you'll ask is, "aren't planes always faster?" The answer depends on your travel distance. If you're journeying 600 miles or less, and are departing from the city center, it may be faster to take the train than to deal with an airport shuttle, airline and baggage check-in, security control, the waiting and boarding time, the flight time, the deplaning, picking up your luggage, finding your way outside, and locating and taking another airport shuttle.

Here are some additional comparisons between the two modes of transportation.

Feelings of safety. People generally feel safer on a train than on a plane, simply because they're on the ground and moving at a slower speed. Secondly, the lack of metal detectors and terrorism/security warnings blaring over the loudspeakers (as is normal in most airports) usually means fewer morbid thoughts crossing your mind.

Overall stress level. Until you become familiar with train travel, it may cause you more stress than air travel. Train stations tend to be very hectic places, with more people in a haphazard rush than you will find at an airport. However, once you're on the train, you're generally able to unwind more and have far more space to move around.

Ability to change plans. If you have a panic attack on your last day in a city and miss your plane to your next stop, you may have to wait until the next day to travel (since many airlines book only one flight per day to a destination) if you can even get a seat – and you will probably lose most of the money you paid for the original ticket. Trains are far more flexible, simply because they're cheaper to run and because reservations often don't need to be made far in advance (or at all).

Urban or Rural?

This book focuses on the stresses facing the urban traveler, because the majority of stressors that lead to panic and anxiety attacks are found in cities: lots of people, too much noise, chaotic traffic, random crime, etc. Whether you choose to vacation in a megacity, a smaller city, a town, or the countryside depends on your personality and interests as well as the type and nature of your anxiety triggers. Here are some things to take into account if you plan to travel through sparsely populated areas.

Attitudes toward mental illness. As we discussed briefly in the last chapter, rural inhabitants tend to have more negative attitudes towards metal illness than urban dwellers. This trend carries across the developing world to the most advanced and progressive nations on the planet. Coming into contact with fewer people means that rural inhabitants generally have less awareness of all the states of the human condition, which usually leads to less understanding, which usually leads to less tolerance. If you think this could be an obstacle to your well-being, don't plan on drifting too far from civilization.

Lack of access to resources. Notwithstanding the attitudes of the locals, you could spend a lot of time worrying about how to access medical resources in isolated areas. Having enough medication with you is critical, and having a travel companion or Professional Travel Companion with you could be important in case you need a drive to the nearest town for a pharmacy or a doctor.

Unknown phobias and fears. If you don't have a lot of experience camping or being outdoors, but choose to come to the boonies just because the big cities scare you off, you could develop new phobias such as fear of open spaces and insects, or be constantly worrying about things like water quality or encroaching wild animals. To avoid planning an uncomfortable experience, ask yourself why you want to vacation in a rural area, and prepare yourself for the physical and psychological challenges before you go.

Adventure Travel

There have been many studies done of mentally healthy adventure travelers who underwent psychiatric changes in the course of their quest. After a week of intense conditions, these travelers suffered disturbed sleep, constant nervousness and vigilance, and paranoia about their surroundings. If people without anxiety disorders suffer such symptoms, then you'll need to be particularly careful about undertaking an activity abroad such as a high-altitude mountain climb, cave exploration, or polar expedition. With this being said, there are some great benefits to adventure travel for anxious people, including:

- Getting out of your head and fully in touch with your senses;

- Intense physical activity to reduce body tension you didn't even know you had;

- A tremendous opportunity for confidence-building; and

- Keeping things simple, with your physical quest your only focus instead of shops, restaurants, entertainers, museums, etc.

Before you get in over your head, literally or figuratively, here are some things to consider about choosing an adventure tour.

Size of the group. Try choosing an adventure travel team of no more than four people, including yourself. This is large enough that your group can take on the great outdoors safely, but not so big that your mental and physical needs are overridden by the group's goal. And if you do have a psychiatric problem or need outside assistance, two people will be able to man camp while the third person helps you regroup.

The impact of physical stress. As we talked about in Chapter 3, there are many physical factors that contribute to panic attacks (and anxiety attacks). Don't let a group of super-athletes push you beyond your limits. Is your contribution to the team always essential, or is there someone who could give you a break if you feel sick from exhaustion or stress?

Inability to practice visualization exercises. If you need to practice cognitive behavioral therapy every day and have been doing the exercises in a controlled environment, think about how successful you'll be practicing the same techniques in a tent (with your team just outside, or possibly inside the tent with you) and when you are tired, dirty, or sore. If you don't think you'll need the exercises while away, discuss the issue more with your psychiatrist.

Potential damage to medications. You're far more likely to accidentally fry, freeze, crush, or turn your medications into a gooey paste during an extreme adventure tour than in the city. If you can't figure out how you'll keep your pills dry, intact, and within the proper temperature range, go to the nearest sports or camping store and ask for suggestions. They may be able to sell you a special vial or temperature-controlled flask.

If just the idea of pitching a tent triggers your anxiety, then read on.

Hotel, Hostel, Bed & Breakfast, or Vacation Rental?
Choosing the right accommodation can make a huge difference in your enjoyment of a trip. Many people only focus on comparing hotels to one another without considering if hostels, Bed & Breakfasts (B&Bs), or vacation rentals might be a better pick for them. We'll go over some advantages and disadvantages of each type of accommodation, and how they can affect your anxiety.

HOTELS
Hotels are hands-down the most typical accommodation you will find. They exist in every country on earth, and while it would be an exercise in frustration to try to group them into simple categories, they do have some common traits, and there are some things in particular to be aware of.

Less interaction with strangers. If the last thing you want is to be bothered by staff or other guests after a day of seeing and interacting with strangers, hotels are the way to book. Everyone is going their own way, and the people at the front desk usually have an innate sense of when to be friendly and when to mind their own business.

Level of security. Hotels usually can't be beat for offering both high-tech surveillance and peace of mind. Many require a key-card to access all but the front doors after ten p.m., and it's almost unheard of anymore to find a room door without a deadbolt. Secondly, many hotels (both mid-range and upscale) tend to cluster together in three- and four-block stretches, which ensures a lot of potential witnesses to problems as well as a lot of security cameras panning up and down sidewalks.

Converted apartments. Converting old apartment buildings into hotels is fairly common in regions that have modernized in the last twenty to thirty years, such as Eastern Europe or Southeast Asia. Unfortunately, behind the new paint and trendy Ikea furnishings are usually paper-thin walls, poor plumbing, and electrical work in need of a major safety upgrade. Furthermore, while you may think that a converted apartment is going to be a suite (or at least large), many old apartments are divided into two or more hotel rooms (which explains the noise problems). You can usually detect a converted apartment hotel by zooming in on the hotel map and finding a bunch of high-rise apartment buildings around it.

HOSTELS

Hostels are famous for their affordability, character, and accessibility; they also have a bad reputation for noise. While it's true that hostel lobbies are typically filled with young people doing anything from strumming guitars to playing ping-pong, the scene upstairs is usually much quieter. Furthermore, most hostels have different floors for back-packer rooms, for double-occupancy rooms, and for single-occupancy rooms. If you book a single occupancy room, it's unlikely that you'll be significantly disturbed since 1) the person next door is staying by themselves, and 2) the rooms are so small that no rowdy guests will fit anyway. If you have a travel companion, the rooms are cheap enough that you can book rooms next to each other, and that's one less neighbor you have to worry about bothering you. Here are some other things to keep in mind.

Reasonably good access. While a hostel certainly offers fewer services than a hotel (and the ones they do offer have to be paid for individually), there's no denying that most hostels are conveniently located. There are plenty right next to train stations and hospitals – bad for the traveler who doesn't want to hear boarding calls and sirens, and good if you need to get back to your room in a hurry, or see a doctor.

Welcome rules and limitations. Many hostels impose a curfew that you'll probably find reassuring to avoid disturbances late at night. If there is no curfew, then there should be mandated "quiet hours" from 10 pm to 8 am. Hostel operators generally aren't shy about enforcing their rules because they're not worried about offending people who are only paying fifty dollars per night.

Presumptions about your symptoms. The biggest concern about staying at a hostel may be the reaction from staff to any anxiety or panic attack symptoms you display. Since hostels see their share of young drifters with party lifestyles – including those searching for a new life as they recover from an alcohol or drug problem – your symptoms may be perceived as complications from an addiction (if you are older, then this is less likely). If questioned by staff, emphasize that you have a pre-existing medical condition, and they'll probably be more than willing to help you.

119

BED AND BREAKFAST INNS (B&Bs)

B&Bs have many of the same amenities as hotels, but on a far smaller and more personal scale since they're usually operated by a couple or a family in their own home. They are often found in rural areas, but also serve urban and suburban areas in many Western countries (or those that were colonized by the British). If the impersonal feel of a hotel leaves you feeling isolated and anxious, and a hostel just isn't the right fit, then B&Bs are a very attractive alternative.

Here are some things to consider:

A little too much like a home. I once stayed at a B&B in Edinburgh, Scotland that made me feel like I wasn't on vacation at all, but had entered someone else's private hell. The operating couple argued each morning about their dog as I tried to enjoy the continental breakfast, and they shared their car problems with their guests. Watching their laundry flutter in the backyard only reminded me of all the chores I'd have to catch up on once I returned home. The second afternoon of my stay, the lady of the house followed me from floor to floor asking about the orange juice stain in my comforter. Knowing that I was being watched most of the time caused me quite a bit of stress.

Perhaps more than with any lodging type, it's important to check traveler reviews of B&Bs before making a reservation. One of the best places to look up reviews is www.tripadvisor.com; B&Bs with as few as three rooms are typically listed.

Familiarity. In many popular destinations where there's no happy medium between five-star luxury hotels and two-star places run by those with limited knowledge of English, a Bed and Breakfast may shine as a beacon of familiarity and comfort. There are a surprising number of B&Bs in places like India, Sri Lanka, and Southeast Asia –

regions that <u>were colonized and heavily</u> influenced by British or Dutch <u>tastes for personable accommodation</u>. You may enjoy the best of both Western and Eastern worlds by staying at a B&B in one of these regions.

Accessible help. The same B&B operators who are a little too much into your business (and not necessarily the ones described above) may be very sympathetic and helpful if you have a psychiatric emergency. Unlike other locals, they may have far more tolerance for the conditions and challenges suffered by foreigners – especially given the number and diversity of people they've willingly let into their house over the years. If you have an attack, you might be offered a free ride to the nearest hospital, or the best information about what local pharmacy to use.

APARTMENT OR HOUSE RENTALS
These are places (usually occupied by a local tenant most of the year) that you can rent by the week or month, without a lot of the distractions found at other accommodations, and without feeling like you're living out of a suitcase. They may be a better pick for social anxiety disorder sufferers, or if you will be staying with two or more family members. Here are some other things to consider.

Independence. Rentals are ideal if you know (or are with someone who knows) an area fairly well, and have the services you need nearby. You're pretty much on your own to get what you need and want – for better or worse. There's no hotel receptionist to offer some casual advice (such as how often the local post picks up, or about any crime concerns in the area), and no one convenient to complain to if the people next door host loud parties all night.

Big commitment. Once you've booked (i.e., paid for) a vacation rental for a week or a month, it's not so easy or cheap to move elsewhere if you're tired or bored (or for more serious reasons). This could be a particular problem if you don't yet understand your preferred pace of travel. For example, three weeks might not sound so long in a place like Paris, but if it's day eight and you've already visited the Eiffel Tower and The Louvre three times, you might want to move on without losing many hundreds of dollars and trying to rearrange airline bookings.

Accompanying PTCs. Renting a house or apartment isn't going to be ideal if you're touring with a Professional Travel Companion, since one of their standard jobs is to stay in the room next to you in case you need or want assistance. Most of the time this would be a locked hotel, hostel, or B&B room, but in a vacation rental this would be just down a private hallway, and could involve some awkward moments when using the bathroom or roaming the kitchen in the middle of the night.

Problematic location. Many vacation rentals are located in mid-town or suburban areas, where (unless you're planning the additional expense of a rental car) you may have to take a taxi or navigate confusing bus lines to get to the main tourist attractions. Furthermore, travel guidebooks will often identify and warn against crime hot-spots in and around hotel and tourist areas, but not other parts of town.

While many rentals are safe and quiet around the clock and around the year, sometimes there's a reason that the tenant family wants to get the heck out of their own home for one or two months a year (such as a seasonal carnival or fair that runs into the wee hours of each night). Ask these types of questions directly of the leasing family before committing.

To search apartment and house rentals worldwide, go to www.vacationrentals.com.

Once you've decided which type of accommodation is best for you, you'll want to find the best you can afford in the area that you plan to stay. Good places to search for hotels, hostels, and B&Bs, as well as read other traveler's reviews, are www.tripadvisor.com, www.priceline.com, www.hotels.com, and www.travelocity.com, or by searching for the name of the chain you're interested in finding abroad.

Professional Travel Companions ✈

A Professional Travel Companion (PTC) is someone you hire to join you on your trip. They are most frequently used to assist handicapped people and those with other significant physical limitations, but they're also hired by highly inexperienced travelers, as well as those who are intimidated or generally fearful of travel (which may or may not include anxiety sufferers). Although many PTCs are "companions" in the true sense of the word, their capacity as an assistant is very broad, and they've been known to coach people with severe anxiety or emotional problems to be able to travel independently. The major drawback is that they tend to be very expensive – effectively doubling or even tripling the cost of your trip. If you're traveling alone and can afford a PTC, you might hire one for your first vacation. You can learn a lot from them about how to travel, and apply the knowledge to future trips you take on your own.

Most PTCs have some medical background, often as a nurse or an emergency medical responder. At the very least they are extensively trained in CPR and first aid. Some set limits on the type of destination they'll travel to (for example, don't expect a PTC with asthma to accompany you to a city with serious air pollution) and many require travel arrangements of at least five days to make it worth their while. Many work with only solo travelers, while others will work with two or more people. Doing an internet search for "professional travel companion" plus the name of your destination country or city will yield a number of websites of PTCs describing their specifications, qualifications, and availability.

A PTC will usually stay at the same place of lodging as you, and travel by the same means of transport. Ordering the necessary air tickets to and from your destination, and picking the destination and duration of your stay, is usually your responsibility. Remember, it's your trip; the PTC is along to help. The PTC should state on their website whether purchase of their services includes their transportation and room and board, or not.

Given the nature of their work, PTCs tend to be extremely adaptable, easy to get along with, and friendly. In many ways they can serve the role of a family member you couldn't or wouldn't bring along because of the inevitable strain it would put on your loved one. Here are some other things to consider.

The interpersonal navigator. If social interactions are a major source of travel anxiety for you, a PTC can take care of a number of those that are necessary to move your trip forward, such as with hotel staff, taxi drivers, or medical clinic receptionists. PTCs are likely to be fluent or semi-fluent in the local language, reducing the chance that you'll be misguided, taken advantage of, or ignored by locals. They can also help expedite your care by explaining your condition to a hospital or doctor in case you have an anxiety or panic attack.

Streetwise. The knowledge and expertise provided by a PTC about such things as local crime, hotel security, how to navigate a large subway system, and how to access the best medical care in a certain area can be invaluable, particularly if you don't trust your own wits yet or are traveling in a developing country.

Experience with mental health disorders. A PTC may be adept at handling physically challenged people, but less familiar in assisting someone with an anxiety disorder. They may not understand what you need, and what aggravates your symptoms. Explain what often leads to your panic or anxiety attacks when interviewing a potential PTC, and see how they respond.

Agree on your plan of action. If you do have an anxiety or panic attack, what role will the PTC have in deciding how to care for you? Go over some scenarios with him or her. You don't want someone who tries to cancel all your reservations if you have a bad day – or waits until you're ready to pass out before offering to help find your pill bottle.

Problem-solving skills. You don't want a PTC who is so focused on being your companion that they forget to apply their common sense and know-how for you. PTCs should be extremely experienced international travelers, with the ability to foresee travel snags, offer you alternatives, and suggest strategies that save you stress, time, money, and risk to your health or well-being.

✗ ***Understand the limitations.*** It may seem obvious, but a PTC can't prevent you from having a panic or anxiety attack. They can't improve your insurance coverage, and they can't tell you why it's important that you travel. They can make many suggestions about what to see and do, but ultimately they can't make you happy. It can be very tempting to turn to a PTC as you would to a therapist or a psychologist, but doing so may lead to strain between the two of you.

Effect on confidence. Ask yourself if having a PTC by your side is going to affect your confidence and self-reliance. It can be easy to grow dependent on a PTC, and once you use one, think that you can't travel without one. Instead, try to learn from your PTC at every turn, and don't be intimidated. Remember that your PTC was once figuring out how to travel with only a single stamp in their passport.

Self-Assessment: Professional Travel Companions
Answer the following questions to see how you feel about PTCs.

What are some reasons you'd want to hire a PTC?

_____

_____

_____

Are there reasons you think you'd be better off without one?

_____

_____

_____

What are some questions you'd ask a PTC before hiring him or her?

_____

_____

_____

How to Communicate Your Anxiety Disorder to a Tour Guide

If you've decided to travel abroad with a tour instead of on your own, with a personal companion, or with a PTC, you should inform the tour representatives about your anxiety disorder and how you manage it. An experienced tour guide will be familiar with assisting people in wheelchairs, on crutches, using oxygen tanks, and the like; they're less experienced at interacting with people who have psychiatric medical conditions, mainly because they don't encounter them as often. This section will help you explain your anxiety disorder to a tour guide, before your trip, without embarrassment or stress. Be reassured that most tour guides are empathetic, open-minded people who will be happy to accommodate you, and that their interest is in everyone having a good time and a safe time. They may also help you avoid or manage anxiety triggers, and get you medical assistance when you need it.

Introduction by email. Once you've purchased a ticket on a travel tour, contact the manager or lead guide by phone or email. Doing so by email can be less awkward, and gives you plenty of time to lay out the facts and your concerns. Reputable tour groups will have a confidentiality policy protecting your private information and will send you, at a minimum, an acknowledgment and confirmation that your email has been attached to your record. You'll usually also receive a personal response and invitation to discuss your conditions, limitations, and concerns in more detail, either by email or phone.

Proper context. It's important to emphasize that your anxiety disorder is an officially diagnosed, preexisting health condition. This will encourage your tour guide to approach you with the same attitude as anyone else with a medical problem, and to utilize the protocols that tour companies have in place for accommodating such guests.

Physical factors. If you're going on an extended tour, or an adventure tour, make sure your tour guide understands that physical factors such as fatigue, nausea, altitude sickness, and others (as discussed in Chapter 3) can contribute to an anxiety or panic attack. They may be able to make or suggest adjustments to your participation in order to minimize physical strain during the tour.

Reassure your tour guide that although you may suffer an anxiety or panic attack, you are proactively managing your condition with medication (and therapy or management techniques, if you feel comfortable sharing that information). If a guide or the tour company perceives that you have an untreated condition, they may suggest (or request) that you don't participate in certain activities in order to protect their liability.

Unpredictability. Make sure the guide understands the unpredictable nature of your disorder. An unfamiliar guide may believe that if you experience something that most people perceive as stressful (such as a visit to an Auschwitz memorial) then you will inevitably have an anxiety attack; the same guide may have a hard time understanding why you would have a panic attack shortly after waking up on a sunny, unremarkable morning.

Reassure the guide that you will not need special medical equipment or supplies (since he or she may be under the impression that you need injections of tranquilizers, or electroshock therapy as part of your treatment).

Mitigating disruptions. Agree with your tour guide on what you will do to prevent a delay to the rest of the group if you have an anxiety or panic attack. Will the guide be able to call an assistant to stay with you while the rest of the tour moves forward?

Travel Insurance and Medevac Insurance

Travel insurance, like any other insurance, is one of those contingencies for managing the "what-ifs" that life may throw your way. It can be expensive, and it often goes unused, but being caught without it can be terrifying and financially devastating. Practicing common sense throughout your journey, picking reliable airlines and hotels, using a lot of hand sanitizer to avoid getting ill, and successfully managing your anxiety from day to day will take you far, but having a travel insurance plan – even a basic one that costs about five percent of your trip – can greatly reduce your anxiety about unforeseen problems and unwelcome surprises.

Most travel insurance plans combine both medical and non-medical coverage. Medical coverage is further divided into 1) provisions for injuries and sudden illnesses such as heart attacks, and 2) provisions for pre-existing medical conditions. General medical coverage (i.e., for sudden illness and accidents) can have considerable overlap with what your Health Maintenance Organization (HMO) or Preferred Provider Organization (PPO) already covers you for, so you'll have to be careful not to buy more than what you need. Non-medical expenses that are usually covered include replacement of lost luggage; reimbursement of your flight costs if your airline declares bankruptcy shortly before you depart; and expenses incurred during travel delays, such as unexpected layovers.

COVERAGE OF PSYCHIATRIC EMERGENCIES

As someone with an anxiety disorder, what will usually be of most concern to you is whether travel insurance covers psychiatric

No7 F. :

What does BC15 cover when you are out of the country.

emergencies. Unfortunately, many affordable travel insurance policies *exclude coverage of pre-existing conditions* – including mental health problems. Furthermore, even those that cover pre-existing conditions usually exclude mental illnesses altogether, including anxiety disorders. The reasons are as frustrating as they are broad, and include:

Regional disparities in diagnosis. We've seen how perceptions of mental illness, and access to care can be quite inconsistent depending on where you are in the world. A hospital in one country could characterize your panic attack, and subsequent ER admission, as treatment for a panic attack, while a hospital in another country could characterize the exact same attack and admission as "a bad case of nerves." These kinds of potential disparities put insurance companies in a difficult position when it comes to reimbursing you, so many just avoid addressing psychiatric illnesses altogether.

Concern about repeat occurrences. Someone who breaks their arm on a trip is very unlikely to come back to the same foreign hospital in a few days with another broken arm. However, someone with a severe anxiety disorder may have repeated attacks, each involving a costly trip to the ER to bring manifestations under control. Think how hard it would be to keep your auto insurance policy after having five accidents in one month, and you can see why travel insurance companies want to protect their pockets by not covering psychiatric illness.

Uncertainty in verifying success of treatment. No doctor can place a cast on or stitch up your anxiety disorder for you. Insurance companies want to receive claims that describe a clear problem (an accident, ulcer, allergic reaction, etc.) and a clear resolution (confirmation from a doctor that your treatment was effective and complete). Their argument is that if there is no documented, physical treatment that took place, then there wasn't enough of a problem to justify your urgent care in the first place.

Before you start looking up travel insurance companies that cover psychiatric disorders, determine if your existing health plan covers treatment of psychiatric illnesses abroad. Your HMO is far more likely to cover you if your attack involves physical complications such as dehydration after vomiting, fainting, or vertigo (in other words, problems that can affect the average person not suffering from an anxiety disorder). HMOs such as Blue Cross or Kaiser Permanente will usually pay "necessary and reasonable" hospital costs abroad for a one-time ER admission, but there's often confusion about what exactly those costs are. Ask some questions, and recognize that transportation to the ER and any follow-up consultations are usually not covered. A PPO will usually offer better coverage in exchange for their higher premiums.

Keep in mind that if you receive medical care in another country, you'll have to pay in cash or with a credit card at the time of service even if you have insurance coverage at home and you know your HMO or PPO will cover your expenses. Because these costs could exceed your credit card limit, be aware that a consular officer at the local embassy may be able to assist in the transfer of funds from the U.S. Note that this is about as much as they can assist with the financial aspect.

It's generally not necessary to notify your HMO or PPO from abroad that you've had emergency treatment; you can notify them when you get home. Reimbursement can take weeks or months, depending on the quality of paperwork you're able to obtain from the foreign hospital, any language barriers, and the type of treatment you've received.

If your HMO or PPO won't cover psychiatric emergencies abroad, here are some travel insurers who (as of early 2013) sell coverage to people with pre-existing conditions, including mental illness:

- All Clear Options: http://www.allcleartravel.co.uk/mental_illness_travel_insurance.html

- Goodtogoinsurance.com: http://www.goodtogoinsurance.com/medical-travel-insurance/travelling-with-a-mental-illness

- The Insurance Surgery: www.the-insurance-surgery.co.uk

- GeoBlue: http://www.overseashealthinsurance.com/global-faq-geoblue.asp

GENERAL TRAVEL INSURANCE

Depending on how well your HMO or PPO covers accidents and illnesses (such as flu, food poisoning, etc.) abroad, you may end up buying two travel insurance plans: one to cover psychiatric illness, and one more general plan. The names of many large travel insurance companies are listed on the U.S. Bureau of Consular Affairs website: http://travel.state.gov/travel/cis_pa_tw/cis_1470.html.

Evaluate any type of general travel insurance for:

- Exclusions or limited coverage for particular regions or countries;

- Coverage of pre-existing physical conditions;

- Whether preauthorization is needed for treatment or hospital admission;

- Whether coverage is renewable from abroad;

- An in-house, worldwide, 24-hour/7-day emergency contact number in English and translation services for health care providers in your destination country;

- Prescription coverage; and

- What the deductibles are, if any.

If you're traveling in a developed country where there is national health care service, you may wonder if you can use the service for free, or if it's cheaper than going to a private hospital. While the latter is usually the case, services are free only for citizens who are residents. If you're a dual citizen of the country, you won't be entitled to free care unless you also have a residence in that country. It's highly unlikely that you'll be turned away; you'll just have to pay the full cost as you would at another foreign hospital.

MEDEVAC INSURANCE

It's highly unlikely that you will need medevac (medical evacuation) insurance to cover an anxiety disorder. Medevac insurance covers the cost of an air ambulance, attending physician or nurse, and care if you're so badly injured or ill that you can't get yourself (or get someone else to transport you) to a hospital. Since urgent treatment for a panic or anxiety attack usually consists of removal from stimuli, checking into a clinic or hospital for relief from acute symptoms, and possibly obtaining medications in addition to what you're already taking, only in extreme cases would you need to rely on a medical evacuation. A lot depends on 1) whether you can simulate a place to rest and recover in an isolated area; 2) whether you can access medications in a remote locale until more formal aid can be reached by standard transportation; and 3) your overall confidence in addressing a psychiatric emergency on your own, or with your group or travel companion.

If you are an adventure traveler – as part of a large group, with a travel companion, or alone – then you may reconsider purchasing medevac insurance. There are plenty of horror stories about travelers who have broken their back or ruptured their appendix in a mountain range or on a small island, and had to pay upwards of $75,000 to be air-lifted to the nearest hospital.

Here are some items to focus on when evaluating a medevac insurance plan:

- Arrangements with hospitals to guarantee payments directly (this reduces the amount of time before your admission);

- Assistance via a 24-hour support center;

- A medical escort (health care provider) to accompany you during evacuation; and

- Coverage of any repatriation costs (i.e., transportation back to your home country). This coverage can add significantly to the cost, so you should consider whether it's necessary or not.

Some other things to understand before you buy are:

Prerequisite travel insurance. A medevac insurer will require proof of travel insurance first, either from them or from another company.

Areas of specialization. Evacuation companies often have better resources and experience in some parts of the world than others. A carrier with a great reputation for mountain evacuations in North

America and Australia, for example, may have only sub-par helicopter service covering the Caribbean.

Ability to choose treatment. Note that medevac insurance may only cover the cost to the *nearest* destination where required care can be obtained. For example, if you need to be evacuated from an accident near the Falkland Islands in the South Atlantic, and you request to be flown into the much larger city of Ushuaia on the Argentine mainland instead of receiving care at the largest port in the Islands, it's possible that your care in Ushuaia won't be covered at all. Verify before purchase whether you'll have any discretion on where you receive care.

The names of many companies offering medevac insurance are available on the U.S. Bureau of Consular Affairs website at http://travel.state.gov/travel/cis_pa_tw/cis/cis_1470.html.

Locating Psychiatric Care Abroad

You should not leave home without researching urgent psychiatric care abroad. While it might sound extremely difficult to find a doctor, a clinic, and their address(es) in a country you've never been to, there are several sources that can help you obtain this information. These include:

1. Your psychiatrist or doctor, who may have established contacts in the country you're visiting;

2. The hotel where you've made your reservation; and

3. The U.S. Embassy website at www.usembassy.gov, which links to hospital listings in dozens of countries and hundreds of cities.

Besides checking with your doctor, the hotel, and the embassy, some other resources to consult (or ask your doctor to consult) include:

- The International Association for Medical Assistance to Travelers (IAMAT), which maintains an international network of hospitals, physicians, and clinics that have agreed to provide care to members while abroad. Listings are among the most comprehensive in the world, and membership is free. Visit www.iamat.org.

- The International Society of Travel Medicine (ISTM), which provides a directory of health care professionals in almost fifty countries around the globe: www.istm.org.

- Travel Health Online, which maintains a list of travel health providers in about thirty of the most popular tourist destination countries: www.tripprep.com.

You're unlikely to find mental health hospitals or facilities in these listings. Remember, you don't want mental health facilities or hospitals since in most countries these are reserved for psychotic individuals, and drug and alcohol addicts. When reviewing the listings, specifically look for facilities offering urgent care or an emergency room, and facilities with a pharmacy. Since you'll rarely need access to any kind of expensive equipment to bring your psychiatric condition under control, you shouldn't be overly concerned if you can only find urgent care facilities instead of facilities with an ER.

We'll talk about the usefulness of travel clinics in the next section, but for the purpose of looking up urgent medical care and physicians, keep in mind that most travel clinics (both in North America and abroad) specialize in providing *preventive* medical care such as vaccinations or altitude sickness medication; they're not one-stop medical shops for a traveler's every need.

Some major hotel chains, including those in developing countries, have in-house physicians who can provide medical care for guests. While it's very unlikely that there will be a psychiatrist on call, a general care physician will be able to meet with you for a fee and write a prescription that you can fill (or have filled) at the local pharmacy that he or she identifies.

Some hotel chains that have in-house doctors include:

- Regents Hotel;
- Park Hyatt;
- The Mandarin Oriental Hotel;
- The Four Seasons; and
- The Ritz-Carlton.

Keep in mind that such hotels are usually affordable to middle-class travelers in countries and regions such as India, Southeast Asia, and Latin America.

If your hotel doesn't have a doctor on call, but you like the idea of being seen in your place of lodging, try going to www.innhousedoctor.com to find a local doctor who makes hotel visits. Hotels may also arrange appointments with local physicians, and for you to be seen in your hotel room.

Be aware that ambulance services are rare in many countries, especially in the developing world, so use whatever form of transport you have to get to a hospital or urgent care clinic. This may include a taxi, or a ride from a hotel employee approved by an onsite manager.

It goes without saying that if you pay for out-of-pocket care, you should obtain and keep copies of all bills and receipts. Do not accept an explanation that the bill will be mailed to you at your home address. If necessary, the U.S. Embassy can help you with such matters. Call them from the clinic or hospital before you leave, and ask them to speak to the medical receptionist.

Finally, you should consider staying in touch with your personal psychiatrist via email or phone while you are abroad. Chapter 10 will go into more detail about how best to communicate with your doctor during a trip.

Medical Checks and Immunizations

The immunizations and vaccinations required to enter a country are usually listed in size-6 font on your group tour ticket or cruise ticket, or on the specific country page linked from http://travel.state.gov. Typical shots needed include those against yellow fever, tetanus, and hepatitis. It's best to print out your list of required vaccinations and bring it to your HMO's travel clinic, and have staff cross-check it to your prescription drugs to ensure that none will interact with your medications.

If you don't have an HMO, try bringing the list of required vaccinations to your local pharmacist and ask them about any interactions with your medications. They may also be able to refer you to an affordable vaccination clinic.

Your travel clinic, or vaccination provider, may tell you to get several immunizations during the same appointment, which you generally shouldn't be concerned about. Before leaving on a trip to Argentina and Uruguay in 2013, my HMO's travel clinic vaccinated me against tetanus, hepatitis, yellow fever, measles, and chicken pox all in the same day. Although it sounded like too many shots to receive at once, I had no issues afterward. Talk to your travel clinic or primary care physician if you're concerned that you are immunocompromised, or are simply overwhelmed at the idea of getting so many shots at the same time.

Be sure to allow plenty of time before your trip to get the vaccinations. The last thing you want is to be a victim of poor timing (many vaccination clinics only operate two-three days per week), arrive at your destination without the immunizations, and risk being detained.

Preparing Your Emergency Contact and Medical Card, and Supplemental Documents

After all your planning, strategizing, researching, and buying any needed insurance, don't forget to prepare and take with you an emergency contact and medical card (or page, printout, etc.) including your critical health and personal data. This shouldn't be left to the last minute since it can take surprisingly long (as in, upwards of ten hours) to gather and list all the information.

Your card should include the names, phone numbers, and addresses or email addresses for the following:

- Family member or close contact remaining at home;

- Your doctor at home, your pharmacy, and your health care provider;

- Travel insurance (and any medevac insurance) information;

- Place(s) of lodging at your destination;

- The U.S. Embassy or consulate in your destination country;

- A list of your medications, including generic and brand names, reason for taking each, dosage information, and how often taken;

- All medical conditions or allergies you have; and

- Documentation of immunizations.

Items to attach or keep with this card include:

- A copy of your medical insurance card (keep the original in your wallet);

- At least one insurance claim form (note that you shouldn't have to navigate through the member services department of your HMO to get insurance claim forms; the travel clinic should carry them);

- A signed letter from your physician describing your general medical condition(s), and all current medications;

- A signed letter from your psychiatrist describing your psychiatric condition(s), and all current medications;

- The list of urgent care services and doctors that you have researched in each country; and

- The name of your disorder, and medications, written in the local languages of the areas you plan to visit. For translation services, try asking your travel clinic first since your psychiatrist or main care practitioner may not know where to send you within your HMO or PPO. Note that it's unwise to use a free online translation service since the software may misunderstand (or not understand at all) complex medical and technical terms and any abbreviations.

Keep the card and all supplemental documents somewhere where they won't get wet or stolen (to be on the safe side, include one copy in your purse or smaller bag, and one in your checked luggage). Tell anyone traveling with you about the card and supplements, and their location(s).

While you're busy compiling all this information, don't forget to fill out the fourth page inside your passport with the name, address, and telephone number of someone to be contacted in an emergency.

Finally, before you go, be sure to register your destination countries, visit dates, and hotel addresses in the U.S Embassy's STEP (Smart Traveler Enrollment Program) system by going to https://step.state.gov/step/. If you do need urgent assistance from an embassy, STEP will already have your basic information on file.

CHAPTER 6

Touring without Stress: How to Leave Your Anxiety in the Baggage Compartment

Once you've put so much thought and effort into planning and preparing for your trip, and have arrived at your destination, your experience as a traveler truly takes flight. This chapter explains how to avoid the stress of being a foreigner by understanding how others see you, and how to overcome problems posed by language barriers. You'll learn how to clue in to your own body language and behaviors to prevent con-artists from taking advantage of you, and how *not* to let your fear of certain situations cause you to take unnecessary risks. We'll address the most common travel anxiety triggers encountered on city streets, how to avoid confrontation, and how to find peaceful (and overlooked) areas in cities when you most need to relax. Read on to understand how to navigate and interact with ease, without trying to be someone you're not, or force yourself beyond your limits.

Joining a Sea of Strangers: A Practical Approach

There are dozens of books you can read on understanding the social norms and etiquette of a particular country you will visit. The amount of information can be overwhelming, and attempts to capture a culture can lead you to believe that millions of people behave similarly in all cultural and social interactions. In reality, etiquette is more rooted in local ways of life, with differences across provinces, rural areas, counties, and even city neighborhoods. Think about how you would answer an American culture question from a Dutchman taking a road trip from Harlem, New York to a small fishing town in Maryland, to New Orleans, and then back to New York City – this time to Manhattan. Would you know where to start?

One of the goals of social norms is to establish standard behavior so that people know what to expect of each other, and can stop thinking so much about basic interactions. While many cultures encourage freedom of expression, many have tolerance "blind spots" and hypocrisies that may have originated in conflicts between religious, social, and political beliefs. Not understanding or respecting social norms, no matter how exasperating they sometimes may be, can lead to feelings of isolation, frustration, dejection, and significant stress, particularly if you're as sensitive as the average anxiety sufferer. The goal of this section is to make you feel comfortable as quickly as possible in a place you've never been, so you can get your mind off "code of conduct" stress and enjoy your trip.

First arrival. Sources of anxiety when arriving to the streets of a foreign city or town may include:

- Not knowing what is appropriate street behavior (voice level, pointing, stopping to make a phone call, etc.);

- Not wanting to offend people (e.g., violating taboos);

- Smaller than normal personal space;

- Level of formality expected or demanded; and

- Fear of confrontation if making a mistake or upsetting someone.

A negative experience can amplify embarrassment into shame, with anger, distrust, and loss of confidence along for the ride. Fortunately, negative experiences and encounters can be mitigated by a few key approaches. These are:

- Observation;

- Self-awareness; and

- Assimilation according to your own comfort level.

We'll go over each of these below.

Observation. Sit at a plaza café or a small park, alone or with your travel partner, and just watch people go by for an hour or so. Notice things such as:

- What are people doing that you find unusual or unnatural?

- What are they *not* doing on the streets that you're used to seeing? This could include activities such as adjusting one's clothes or hair, blowing one's nose, or snacking at a pedestrian stoplight

- How do other people react to someone who engages in generally anti-social behavior (such as letting a door slam in a stranger's face, or corralling a taxi that someone else has hailed?)

Self-awareness. Realize that you have two different street behaviors: one when you're at home, in your accustomed environment, and one as a tourist or outsider. At home you're used to being part of the scene around you; as a tourist, you're usually preoccupied with the scene, and stand apart from it. You may walk more slowly, stare, stop suddenly, and meander or change direction. You may be more polite and more patient than normal, and you may be louder or quieter than normal. Your "tourist" behavior may or may not be more suited to the mannerisms of those around you. Ask yourself:

- How many of your unassuming street behaviors are going to draw unwelcome attention?

- How good are you at controlling your first impulses and responses?

- How much will this matter in your particular environment?

Comfortable assimilation. Trying to blend in *too* much with the locals may take a lot of the enjoyment out of your travel. Hurrying, looking down instead of around, and constantly restraining your interest and curiosity aren't anyone's idea of a nice tour. Identify which two or three of your habits are the most disruptive or displeasing, and make a regular effort to tone them down. Remember, the goal is to spare yourself embarrassment and anxiety – not make yourself uncomfortable.

Establishing Straightforward Relationships as a Foreigner: Understanding Types of Interactions, and Roles

TYPES OF INTERACTIONS

It might be unnerving to think about negotiating with strangers for what you need and want on a trip. Asking for help, receiving services, or making arrangements with people you don't know can expose you to a wide range of personalities, moods, cultural differences, and the occasional thoughtless or rude response. As a traveler, it helps to view your interactions as falling into one of two categories: 1) those that you have to initiate, and 2) those that the other person has to initiate. Another way to think of these respective categories is:

1. Those interactions that you can't control, and

2. Those that you can.

Generally, if you're paying for a service, then someone else has to initiate the interaction – and will likely do so in a courteous and sensitive manner. Since as a tourist you are paying for a number of things including hotels, airfare, secondary transportation, and meals, the majority of your interactions will be those where the other person must approach you and offer what you need and want. Understanding this can go a long way towards mitigating your anxiety since breaking the ice with someone is almost always the most stressful aspect of an interaction. Let tour guides, waiters, bellhops, maids, flight attendants, and hotel receptionists do their jobs, and relax.

Examples of interactions that *you* usually initiate include those with taxi drivers; when asking for directions or help; when making reservations or arrangements you haven't yet paid for; or with unresponsive service staff. If you're like most anxiety sufferers, you try to keep these interactions to a minimum – or resort to email for reservations or to file a complaint. Chapter 10 will go over these interactions in more detail.

There are several scenarios where either you or another person may initiate an interaction, such as with store clerks, police or security, other guests, or other tourists. In some cases you'll want or need something enough that you'll broach someone whether it causes you anxiety or not; in other cases, someone may notice that you need something, or are having problems, and come to you. You'll have to decide whether it causes you more stress to approach someone out of the blue, or wait a while to be approached.

Is there a correlation between how much money you spend and how much thought you have to put into interacting with others? Not necessarily. Although budget travelers are going to pay for fewer services and have to be more proactive in getting what they need, people who are traveling in luxury are going to have more discretion in their interactions with a large number of service people, and may spend a lot of time and energy concerned about how much to tip, who to call for a certain type of service, etc. Things are going to be most straightforward for middle-of-the-road travelers.

ROLES YOU PLAY *N7*

There are basically three roles you play as a tourist. These are:

1. Customer;

2.   Guest in country; and

3.   Fellow tourist.

Once you realize that this is how others see you, you may lose a lot of fear of interacting with others. Here are some things to be aware of regarding each of your roles.

Customer. Despite your status as a paid customer at a hotel or on a flight, train, ship, etc., you might encounter some unwarranted negativity from service people that causes you distress. It may seem obvious, but different service people will have different attitudes toward tourists.   Many are in their jobs because they enjoy interacting with people around the globe; others are frustrated with working for low wages, and resent that you have the means to vacation thousands of miles away.

If you're stuck in a days-long arrangement with stress-inducing service staff, try softening them up by getting their mind off work. You can usually do this by talking about what you love about their city, compared to what you don't like at home. Frustrated people want to rediscover their surroundings, or see that they have things better than they realized – and curiosity about what your home country is really like often gets the better of their unfriendliness.

Guest in country. If you wander off the typical tourist path, you may interact with the people of your host country outside of just the service sector. This could be at a supermarket, a bus stop, or a post office, where – depending on how provincial your destination is – you could be stared at or treated as something of a novelty. Friendly and curious people can cause you to feel very awkward without intending to.   If their attention or scrutiny causes you anxiety, remember that you have a lot of control at the start of an interaction with someone, but the longer you engage, the less you're able to deny invitations or queries without stress. Do your share of smiling and excusing yourself – and move on with your business.

There are plenty of stories about Americans (and a lot fewer about Canadians) who are openly derided or snubbed abroad, but if you're traveling alone or with only one other person, you're far more likely to be judged as an individual rather than subject to stereotypes. Some of the personality traits that are common among anxiety sufferers, such as being reserved and sensitive to the needs of others, work against the usual stereotypes applied to Americans, and in your favor.

Fellow tourist. You're more likely to have an unpleasant experience with other tourists than with service personnel or locals. This is because you're essentially competing with other tourists for the best seats, space, or attention wherever you go. People from different cultures may demonstrate a variety of impatient or aggressive responses when it comes to seeing what they want to see, and going where they need to go. Keep in mind that your public behavior may be equally unfamiliar to them, and may even come off as arrogant or threatening, even if this is the last thing you intend and you're behaving like you always would.

Despite these challenges, you should be prepared to occasionally interact with other tourists to get what you need or want. You may need to use someone else's phone because your battery has gone dead, or you could need a couple bills of the local currency because the local TravelExchange kiosk doesn't open for hours. The basic rule is to not expect any favors from other tourists. If you need something, you should have something to offer in exchange. This could be, for example:

•   Your still-valid metro ticket in exchange for someone's map;

- A camera trade to take pictures of each other in front of landmarks; or

- A couple Euros in exchange for using their cell phone for a few minutes.

Making it clear what you have to offer, and what you would like in exchange, makes it difficult for the other person to say no, yet doesn't make you come off as pushy or demanding.

Taking the Stress Out of Language Barriers

One of the first things someone might ask when you announce your trip to another country is, "Do you know the language?" Unless you're visiting an ancestral homeland, are a language buff, or have learned foreign language(s) for your job or personal reasons, the answer will likely be no. You may suffer anxiety over the thought of being unable to make your way around or communicate your needs during your trip. The more this anxiety builds, the more pressure you could put on yourself to spend many hours learning a language – including nuances that you're unlikely to need. Furthermore, if you're visiting several countries and a different language is spoken in each, you could be setting yourself up for overload and frustration and may even think about delaying your trip.

Unless you're planning to spend an extended amount of time in a country, knowing the hundred or so "quick reference" words and phrases in a standard travel language book will usually be sufficient to get you around. Focus on language concerning transportation, directions, obtaining assistance, and health and safety issues (such as the words for *danger, caution,* and *hospital,* as well as how to ask for an embassy or the police). If this still doesn't sound like enough, remember that there's a reason that so many travel language books are sized to fit in your pocket. You can look up phrases and words as you need them, without putting yourself through painful memorization exercises weeks before your trip.

Do You Speak English?

This is an essential phrase to know in every language spoken in the places you're visiting. It manages your limited language skills while showing that you're culturally sensitive enough to not just assume that someone speaks your language; it also helps break the ice. If the person confirms that they speak English, then you've started off on the right foot; if they say no, then nod or apologize (think of how you feel when you dial the wrong phone number) and move on to someone else. If you can't move on to someone else, see how far you can get with numbers and gestures. If you're still struggling, then other employees or passersby are likely to notice, and chances are one of them will step in to help – if for no other reason than to show off their command of English.

A word of caution: if you have a rudimentary grasp of a foreign language and ask for directions or check into a hotel in that language, you need to be able to understand the person's response. The person might answer at a mile a minute, and you'll either pretend to understand and move on, or ask for clarification in English – at which time the person will wonder (with some frustration) why you didn't ask in English in the first place. If you're not proficient enough to go back and forth in conversation on a particular topic, then it would be best to ask *Do you speak English?* and go from there.

Addressing the Most Common Anxiety Triggers While Touring
Part of the fun of traveling is getting to explore the unknown. Unfortunately, the delight of discovering something new and different can sometimes come with significant distractions and aggravations – what you and I know as anxiety triggers. Addressing and managing several of the most pervasive travel anxiety triggers is easily possible, and will help you get back to enjoying your trip.

Detours. The more you travel, the more you'll realize that the world is an unfinished work of art. The average metropolis can have at least half a dozen construction projects shaking the ground at once, while a mega-city can have a dozen or more. Popular tourist destinations become even more popular and congested when they win a bid to host a major sporting event, or cultural or political summit; new coliseums, arenas, hotels, and rail tracks suddenly spring from the dirt, outdating your map and giving you a new challenge in the form of blocks-long rows of pylons and yellow tape. Although construction detours are the most common you will find, you might also encounter detours to accommodate marches, protests, security lockdowns for government officials, biking and marathon events, and others.

Unfortunately, pedestrian detours can lead to confusion, disorientation, and getting very, very lost if you don't know how to handle them. Your stress level is going to shoot sky-high if you "follow the orange signs" only to find yourself in an alley at dusk with no idea which direction to turn. Here are some useful guidelines for managing detours.

1. Trust the logic of the detour. City planners and engineers have to get a number of high-level approvals to implement one, and while not all detours are intuitive, the basic goal is to get you as close as possible back to where you need to be, in the shortest amount of time. You may have to let go of your initial assessment of where you *should* be, and go with the flow of a detour even if it feels like you're going the wrong way. As any construction worker would tell you, there's a reason why two U-turns gets you headed in the right direction again.

2. Before you go through the detour, clearly understand where you are by picking a landmark that you can identify from blocks away (i.e., at the end of the detour). This is essential if you need to retrace your steps, but the detour only allows foot traffic one way (this usually occurs with detours from a train or metro station).

3. If you have no idea where you've ended up at the end of the detour, see where the majority of other people (especially commuters) are going, and follow them. Tourist areas in most cities back right up to central business districts. If you still can't

find the tourist area or where you want to go, and it's too stressful to ask a stranger, then head back to the detour exit and try another direction. Improvising *after* you've followed a bunch of people two blocks down the road is not a good idea.

4. Recognize that detours can take you up or down as well as north, west, east, or south. You may have to take stairs, tunnels, or escalators to avoid a construction zone. If you think only in terms of traveling *across*, you could find yourself staring at a dirty wall.

Crowds. There's nothing like a throng of humanity crammed into a small plaza or a narrow street to aggravate even the most extroverted of anxiety sufferers. Anxiety triggers include noise, getting jostled around, fear of pickpockets and other thieves, and feelings of constant self-consciousness. Some people are bothered by the perceived indifference and aggressiveness of a crowd, while others worry about having a panic or anxiety attack in front of so many people.

The key to dispelling anxiety about crowds is to understand that they're made up of smaller units of people. In social settings, people rarely interact in groups larger than six or seven, and are so tuned in to each other that they won't even notice you. Except at private functions, each group knows very little about anyone outside their group. And each group can look cliquish simply because *they're* a little uncomfortable about all the strangers around them.

As a tourist, managing a crowd (i.e., bunches of groups) is usually a matter of either getting around it, or through it. Groups in dining halls, plazas, or other confined settings can be the most challenging given the potential to get "stuck" for space between one group and another. You'll find that walking the perimeter of a gathering area can be less stressful as you reduce the number of times you have to break "through" people, and are simply going around them.

Crowds in line are often less intimidating. People will pay attention to you at the beginning, for long enough to see if you're going to cut in front of them; otherwise, their attention will be diverted to how fast they're moving forward.

A third type of crowd gathers to fill a theater, stadium, or other event venue; their focus is on what's happening in front of them, not on you. Take a look around the rows and you'll see that people are too absorbed to watch you. If you still feel considerable anxiety being part of an audience, then sit in the back (or towards the top) where you won't feel so many pairs of eyes staring at the back of your head.

Doppelgangers. Given the sheer number of people you'll see when you're a tourist, you may glimpse someone who intensely resembles someone you know, or knew, which can cause sudden and disturbing flashbacks. This is a particular problem for people with PTSD, but can also affect other anxiety sufferers. Upon seeing the lookalike, your mind struggles to put an ex-lover, old friend, teacher, or relative in the context in front of you, and you can get quite disoriented in the process. Your sense of time and distance are compromised and your mind's fixation on particular memories can result in physical symptoms that lead to an attack.

Following a lookalike to see how he or she differs from someone you know (or knew) may only cause you more distress. Instead, try to re-immerse yourself in the present as quickly as possible. You might talk about it with your travel companion; most people have experienced seeing a disturbing "double" before. If you're traveling alone, try making a quick call home to family and friends. Without even knowing it, they'll remind you of who is part of your life now, as well as where you will find them.

Eye contact. One of the most unnerving things for a traveler with an anxiety disorder is to pass, see, or be passed by hundreds or even thousands of strangers every day – many of whom, for whatever reason, want you to look back at them. Stressful emotions that arise from unwanted eye contact include feelings of intimidation from being stared down; intense self-consciousness from people who sneer for no good reason; uneasiness from sexually suggestive ogling or once-overs; and the glares or grimaces of angry or sad people. People carry a tremendous amount of emotional energy in their gaze, and making eye contact with every single person you come near could be so draining that you're distracted from sightseeing.

One of the reasons people think they need to make eye contact is to avoid bumping into others. The truth is, you don't have to make eye contact in order to navigate sidewalks, shops, squares, and tourist attractions; if you look in the direction you want to go, then people will not bump into you. Even if you have sunglasses on people will generally be able to tell by your body language what direction you plan to steer, since both your body and attention tilt slightly (but perceptibly) depending on what you're focusing on. You can make a similar evaluation of others by doing a split-second assessment of their focus and movements.

Is avoiding eye contact a way of giving into (or developing) a phobia? Given the number of cultures that discourage direct eye contact between people on the street – and particularly between the opposite sex – it would be difficult to say yes. Save the emotional energy it takes to make eye contact for the people who matter more – hotel staff, store clerks, and others who are helping you have a pleasant journey.

Perceived sounds of distress. People with anxiety disorders have often experienced a significant trauma in their past. Certain noises, particularly screaming and shrieking, can cause you great alarm and induce sweating, heart palpitations, and other physiological manifestations. If you suffer from this phobia, screaming is not an expression of a good time, but a sign of an emergency. Screaming children at play can make you think someone is hurt; screaming women may haunt you with images of sexual assault.

To keep a panic reaction from escalating, take a quick look at what screaming children or women are doing, and observe other people's reactions to them. If there was really something wrong, wouldn't others notice and step in to help?

In general, someone else's noise rarely has anything to do with you. If it's still a significant anxiety trigger, try to stay away from amusement parks, carnivals, and other places where you're most likely to hear excitement bordering on terror.

Accidents. Seeing an accident while touring – whether it involves a slip, trip, fall, or a vehicle – can jar your confidence and make you feel like you're next to have disaster descend upon you. Depending on how much you can relate to the person who suffered the accident, and just how bad it was, you may put sudden limits on your physical activities or transportation that can rapidly develop into a phobia. There are some things to understand about accidents before your healthy precautions build into a cage of fear.

I once saw a middle-aged tourist do a full somersault down the departures escalator at London's Heathrow Airport. He was distracted by writing on the luggage tag of his carry-on bag, and lost his balance as the escalator belt hit a bump followed by a small jerk. The next thing the man knew he'd flipped upside down, and then lay dazed on his tailbone on the bottom step.

Interestingly, about half the people at the scene (the ones who hadn't seen him writing up his luggage tag, completely oblivious to his surroundings) were shocked and horrified; the others (who'd seen what the man had been doing) had a look on their faces like, "Well, what did he expect?"

The point is that most of the accidents you see or hear about – perhaps of a taxi driver backing into a tourist, or of someone twisting their ankle between cobblestones – are not true "accidents," but *mistakes*. An accident implies that nothing could be done to prevent the incident from happening, when really a lot could be done in most cases – if people were paying attention and taking the proper precautions. Once you realize this, and understand that it takes two people, places, or things to have an "accident," the less anxiety you will suffer. Instead of blaming an elevator or a door or a moving vehicle, you recognize that by being vigilant you not only make up for hazards and for other people's carelessness, but you give yourself a lot more control over your surroundings.

Avoiding Confrontation While Taking Photographs

If you're a visual person and want to relive many moments of your trip, then taking pictures will be one of the most rewarding and essential parts of your journey. Unfortunately, it's the one thing you do in the normal course of touring that can cause some provocation – usually because people are concerned that they've appeared in your photo (or video footage). In general, the more elaborate your camera is, the more attention you're going to attract using it. Snapping shots with your cell phone is going to draw the least attention; setting up a tripod with a camera the size of your head will attract a lot more; and walking around with a videocamera constantly raised and pointing will attract the most.

You may be aware of all of this, and have reluctantly resolved to hold back your shutterbug impulses. However, there's no need to restrict yourself like this, and later regret what you didn't get on film. Here are some tips to avoid confrontation and ease anxiety when out and about with a camera.

Portray clear intentions. If you want to photograph a famous landmark and there are people constantly milling around, look directly at what you're shooting and don't make eye contact with the people around it. This will reassure others that you're not interested in them or in invading their privacy.

If someone confronts you about whether you've taken a picture of them, or included them in your shot or video footage, offer to erase the photo. In almost every case they won't actually take you up on this; they just want some reassurance that you're a tourist and not a voyeur. If they do take you up on it, then wait until they're out of the picture, so to speak, and re-shoot. It's a lot faster than arguing with someone and getting yourself significantly distressed.

Watch what others are doing. If there are signs or graphics around a place indicating that photography isn't allowed, take a look at whether others are shooting photos anyway. I have been in museums or churches that officially ban photography (and state so right on the front door), yet people were taking pictures left and right and no one stopped them. If you want the same picture everyone else is taking, then take it. The worst that can happen is that a grounds person comes by and chastises the whole lot of you.

The opposite can hold true for military buildings and embassies. Military buildings can be surprisingly difficult to recognize, and it's usually understood that absolutely no pictures can be taken even if there are no signs indicating such. Embassy districts are usually filled with attractive buildings and landscapes that make for great picture opportunities, but keep in mind that they often prohibit photography as well.

Here are some other guidelines:

- In poor areas where local or indigenous people depend heavily on tourists for economic survival, check to see if you're expected to pay to take a photograph (of a person, place, or item). Save yourself embarrassment and stress by abiding by the rules.

- In certain countries, men should be careful not to include women or children in their photographs, even in crowded areas and when the subjects are oblivious.

- If you want to take simple action photos to capture the spirit of a place and time (with no concern about the quality of the photos) try "shooting from the hip," i.e., snapping pictures without a particular focus on the subject. This is useful for photographing crowded places like carnivals and festivals without attracting the attention of those around you, or stopping in the middle of a congested area to raise your camera to your face.

Stressed? Watch Your Body Language: How to Protect Yourself from Those Looking for "Easy Targets"

People who prey on others for a living don't have a hard time picking an anxious or distressed person out of a crowd. You may appear unusually bothered by solicitors in street malls, or visibly steer away from loud noise or people. Anxiety sufferers tend to have quicker, uncontrolled reactions and jerky movements; they also tend to overreact in order to protect themselves from real or perceived threats. Thieves love this behavior because it indicates you're more tuned into distractions than to your belongings or your overall environment. Thieves want to victimize someone who (1) won't notice they've been ripped off or otherwise taken advantage of, and (2) in the event that they do notice, either won't put up a fight, or will overreact and lose their credibility to passersby or police.

Here are some specific antics and mannerisms that help thieves identify an easy target. How many of these do you exhibit in public?

- Checking your bag or purse repeatedly for items you think you've misplaced

- Openly taking pills

- Looking up and down instead of around or straight ahead

- Hugging yourself or hunching forward

- Generally looking flustered, unorganized, disengaged, or overwhelmed

The goal of avoiding a pick-pocket or other scam artist is not so much to protect your money, but to spare you the trauma of an incident. Being victimized can quickly lead to hypervigilance, fear of leaving your hotel room, and a panic or anxiety attack once you realize what you've lost (or how you've been deceived). We won't go over all the different ways that thieves can take advantage of you, but focus on how to make you appear (and therefore *be*) far less of a target.

Project confidence and strength. It's not what you feel inside, but how you walk, look, and move that makes a difference. Do you shuffle along like you're trying to get away from (or hurry towards) something? Change how you walk by pushing more from the balls of your feet; you'll feel like you're reaching up and out instead of just moving forward. In doing so, you'll look taller, bigger, and stronger.

Earlier in this chapter we talked about eye contact. There's a difference between *avoiding* eye contact and *not making* eye contact. If you feel you're being followed or watched by someone, look at them without making eye contact. Troublemakers don't like having a wary eye on them.

Increase personal space. Don't be afraid to take up space when you stand or walk. Anxious people have a reputation for being pushovers, literally. If you let yourself get shoved aside, not only do you look intimated, but you actually set yourself up for someone to come in too closely and empty your pockets. Part your legs, and let your arms swings a little so that people give you a few extra inches of space on either side.

Get yourself ready to go out. Before you actually step onto the sidewalk, make sure you've taken your latest pill dose, and that you have all your belongings where you expect to find them. Resist being rushed out of a hotel, taxi, or restaurant just to make room for the next guest; don't hurry out of souvenir stores with your wallet in one hand and your bag of gifts in the other. If you need to look at a map or directions, pick a quiet place to sit down and do so. The more organized you are and the more sure you are of where you're going, the more you'll feel at ease and not exhibit distressed body language.

Managing the Impacts of Derealization

Derealization is a phenomenon of feeling distanced from your surroundings, either physically, mentally, or emotionally. It can affect anyone, but is especially prominent among anxiety sufferers. Derealization is your mind's way of protecting you from extreme emotions and overstimulation, and is often accompanied by wooziness, muted hearing, and a feeling of slight intoxication. Many mentally healthy people have a hard time explaining it, and may describe it as "living in a fog" or "losing a grip on reality." It's smart to recognize that derealization is a self-protective mechanism, but to also know when to push yourself through the "fog" so you can fully enjoy all the sights, sounds, and experiences of traveling.

Here are some derealization effects you may experience while touring, and what to do about them.

Compromised navigational ability. Derealization can cause you to perceive your surroundings as "flat" or two-dimensional, which usually compromises your sense of space, perspective, and direction. You may find yourself going around in a big circle because your mental "compass" (which gives you a rough estimate of how much time has passed and ground you've covered) isn't working as it should.

To manage this, you might take advantage of internet sites such as Google Maps (www.google.com/maps) that allow you to virtually "place" and move yourself on the ground in thousands of locations around the world, and view what the actual streetscapes look like. Having a good sense for the layout of a city days or weeks before you go can free some of your mental energy to enjoy yourself at your destination, and care for your personal safety.

Autopilot. Unintentionally lapsing into autopilot is one of the most frustrating impacts of derealization, since getting "stuck" in one mode means you're unable to fully process, acknowledge, or appreciate your surroundings. Basically, you become indifferent to the range of behaviors and responses of the people and things around you. Sufferers report a feeling of fatalism about anything they do, i.e. that they have no role in their environment, and no free will even though the present and future are shaped in real time. These feelings can quickly lead to sadness, depression, and questioning the worth of your trip.

If you're suffering from a chronic case of autopilot, you've taken the first step in managing it just by recognizing it. Next, find a quiet place to sit down and just look around for a while, consciously focusing on different things than normal. Remember that derealization is a defense mechanism, so try to identify the perceived threats in your environment. Is avoiding any spontaneous reaction to them causing you to miss out on a number of pleasurable observations around you? If so, is there a way to turn perceived threats into more positive challenges?

Short-term memory problems. Because derealization pulls you out of the immediate environment and into a "safer" place inside your mind, you could have difficulty processing real-time information since your brain views it as auxiliary to your preoccupations (i.e., your "fog"). For many people this manifests in an inability to remember a train number, address, or directions even if you can visualize where and from whom you got the information. This can cause you stress and embarrassment if you have to come back to the same service person and ask them to repeat such basic details.

If having a short-term memory problem is a great source of frustration to you, you might put yourself at risk of developing compulsive tendencies by repeating numbers, addresses, or sentences in your mind. A better solution is to carry around a small notepad and pen and jot down the information you need as you get it. This might be viewed as slightly eccentric, but will not attract a lot of attention.

Compromised physical self-awareness. A final effect of derealization is difficulty in relating and responding to your physical environment. Because you're not fully present mentally or emotionally, you're not paying much attention to potential hazards around you. You may even feel like there's no "boundary" between you and your surroundings; some people report a sense of transparency, or floating. If you suffer from this, be very careful at transportation points and on busy streets. You could find yourself standing right in the middle of a bus lane or two feet from trolley tracks without even noticing – with potentially disastrous consequences.

If you have a hard time noticing street signs because you're more attuned to other visuals, then train yourself to observe where other people are congregating, and follow them to safety. It's better to kill time with loud or irritating people than to have a serious accident.

Don't Let Anxiety Steer You: Addressing Challenges Head-on Instead of Taking Unnecessary Risks

Anxiety often causes you to avoid confronting questions about the challenges, realities, and complications you face in life, and this tendency can be very problematic when traveling. You can develop mental blocks instead of questioning the variables and "what-ifs" in front of you, just because the consequences of something going wrong are too stressful to think about. It may seem obvious to say this, but just because you dread thinking about something doesn't mean it will go away.

Here are some examples of blindsiding yourself that can lead to stressful incidents abroad:

- Making too many assumptions about a place, event, or situation because you're too embarrassed or nervous to ask someone for clarification;

- Leaving essential details to chance; and, of course,

- Getting lost because you are too afraid to ask for directions.

Here are some skills and approaches to help you avoid taking unnecessary risks while traveling.

Asking for assistance. There are times when you're not going to have full control over your circumstances or schedule, and will require assistance to get from Point A to Point B. Examples include:

- Making a tight flight connection when your first plane is running late;

- Arriving at your reserved hotel only to be told that it's closed due to a sanitary issue, and that you've been rebooked at another hotel a half mile away; and

- Being pulled off a train at a border checkpoint and told to board a bus two blocks away to get to your final destination.

These types of things happen far more often than you might care to think, but under no circumstances should you think you'll be stranded, have to run like hell, or have to swallow a major inconvenience. Any company, chain, or customs official who tells you to make an adjustment is obligated to assist you, even though they may not be helpful or forthcoming with information. You should *not* succumb to pressure to leave your current plane, hotel, or train by being told that instructions will be given to you at the other end. Ask the person who orders the change every question you can think of; request written instructions, and obtain phone numbers if possible. For a tight plane connection, request to disembark the plane before everyone else, and ask the flight attendant for exact directions to the gate of your next flight.

Evaluating a situation. Assessing the *who, what, when, where, why,* and *how* of an unfamiliar scenario takes patience and a level head, and you may not have much of either if the stresses of travel are getting to you. In order to stop thinking about something (i.e., avoid grappling with all the details of several possibilities) you may choose the most convenient or least confrontational solution to a problem without understanding all of the ramifications. You may also jump to conclusions if it's difficult and uncomfortable to assess all the facts.

If this is an issue for you, then write out the pros, cons, and unknowns of a particular scenario. The physical act of writing something out slows your thoughts down, and a problem can look surprisingly different on paper than it does in your head. You might also share your situation and response with someone who isn't involved (such as a hotel receptionist or shop owner) without necessarily inviting their help or opinion. If their first comment is that your plan sounds too cheap, fast, or easy, then it probably is, and you should think things through better before acting.

Ability to prioritize. In a foreign environment it's easy to develop "tunnel vision." Without your home, job, and many of your loved ones present to remind you that your safety and mental health come first, you may let your travel goals influence careless decisions that can take a serious toll on you. For example, on your final vacation day, you might rank seeing the last beautiful park in a city over getting dinner and giving yourself a chance to unwind, because the thought of spending hundreds of dollars to come back to see the park another time is overwhelming. If you find that you're running yourself down just to tick an extra item or two off your tour list, then you're most likely not enjoying your vacation – meanwhile, you're setting yourself up for a breakdown if you don't pay attention to your essential needs.

Assumptions about availability. Recognize sooner than later that money and space rule logistics when it comes to travel, and that unless you have a receipt or other confirmation, you're probably not going to get what you want. For example, you might need to take a hotel airport shuttle the morning you check out, but because it causes you stress to talk to an unfriendly receptionist, you don't confirm if reservations are needed on the shuttle or not. The next morning you find yourself denied a seat on the full shuttle, and you end up missing your flight because you lost your composure and forgot that you could call a taxi.

Even friendly and well-meaning service people can inadvertently or carelessly mislead you. Their managers know this, which is why important instructions and reservation information are usually included in the fine print of any service. Request and read what you'll need to know.

Assumptions about accessibility. If you're confident that you can walk all over a city to see what you want, make sure pedestrian access is available on your planned routes. While maps don't necessarily lie, most of them are designed for drivers, and following a smooth white line down your map could get you marooned on a concrete street divider or trapped at the entrance of a six-lane highway tunnel. A major warning sign that your nice sidewalk will turn into a freeway ditch is seeing an airport, dam, or industrial rail hub on the map adjacent to your walking path. Before undertaking a walk longer than about two miles, email or ask your hotel receptionist if your route is pedestrian-friendly. You can save yourself a minor meltdown from putting yourself at great physical risk in an unfamiliar area.

Assumptions about consistency. You may take for granted where you live that transportation access is straightforward and predictable, and that municipal and commercial services are distributed reasonably well across a given area. This consistency is lacking in many places around the world, due to 1) environmental considerations, 2) damage caused by past wars, 3) poor political decisions, or 4) simply an oversight by the transportation or land-use planning departments. Quirks in train and bus service can literally take you for a ride if you don't verify exactly where you're going and how to get back, and elitist municipal habits such as building all the parks in the city's rich areas will leave you wondering where the heck you can sit down to take a break. Other examples of consistency gone awry include:

- A return bus stop a full two blocks down the street from where you got off

- Trains that run every half hour in the morning, and then every three hours when you need to leave the city

- A metro line that serves the north and west suburbs very well, but doesn't even exist in the south and east

- Three pharmacies all within seven blocks of each other, and then none for miles

You can get yourself bitterly lost, frustrated, and psychologically worn down looking for services that simply don't exist, or are where you'd least expect to find them. Once you acknowledge that exceptions are a fact of life on the road, you'll be a savvier and less distressed traveler.

How to Find a Quiet Spot Almost Anywhere

Have you ever heard someone come back from a trip and say they need a vacation to recover from their vacation? They usually feel that way because they didn't let themselves decompress at any time while they were away. Given the greater emotional and physical energy exerted during a trip, both mentally healthy people and those with anxiety disorders can feel drained or overstimulated during and after travel. It's often harder to give your mind and emotions a break than to give your body a break, but it's particularly critical for you to block a morning or afternoon every few days to unwind and think about how what you just saw or did fits into your overall life – or perhaps to not even think at all, but just let your mind wander. Finding a tranquil place to relax and regroup is the easiest way to do this.

Unfortunately, traditional "quiet" places may turn into anything but if everyone else decides to go there for their own relaxation. Think of oceanside cafés that get so loud you can't hear the waves washing up; well-known churches that sound like malls inside; and parks that put you in the path of an impromptu tag game – hardly anyone's idea of peace.

Don't think you have to return to your hotel room mid-day, or wander into an isolated and potentially dangerous area in order to regroup. Here are a few universal, but often overlooked, places to unwind.

Botanical gardens. These can sound like a bore to those not interested in plants, but botanical gardens have all of the relaxing characteristics of parks, but because of the (usually) small entrance fee, attract a different crowd; your chances of encountering skateboarding teenagers, drunks, or soccer practice are slim to none. Botanical gardens are not unique to North America and Asia; you can find them in even the poorest and most remote countries in the world. There's no shortage of places to sit down, and you can generally stay as long as you want after paying the day's admission.

Universities. Many universities have the look and feel of self-sustaining villages, and you'd have a hard time finding one without some green areas and benches (and often a pond and some wildlife). Frat and sorority houses aren't very common outside of North America, and while there's obviously going to be plenty of activity on the main thoroughfares on weekdays, the overall atmosphere – especially on weekends – is subdued. Another plus is that many universities are easily accessed within metropolitan areas, and even the grounds of most private universities are open to anyone.

Zoos. You'd be hard pressed to find a zoo without an attractive, natural setting – and interacting with (or just watching) animals can quickly pull you out of your head and back into the moment. About half of all major world cities have a zoo within three miles of tourist areas. Try visiting on a weekday evening, or mid-afternoon after school groups have cleared out.

Embassy areas. These neighborhoods are particularly prominent in capital cities, and are often in easily accessible areas. Although there aren't many places to sit down, they are certainly a great place for a quiet stroll. Embassy neighborhoods are rarely crowded, aesthetically pleasing, and you can let your guard down because security is second to none.

Stationed trains. Particularly in European cities, long-distance trains pull into a station well before departure – by an hour, and sometimes more (especially if your city is the route terminus). A parked train can be a very peaceful alternative to trying to rest your mind and feet in the chaotic main station hallway. I've done it many times and not been bothered by attendants or conductors (unlike airplanes, which are usually swept and cleaned after every flight, the usual train is only serviced at the end of the day).

Obviously, you need to make sure the train doesn't roll away taking you someplace you don't want to go, but the chances of this happening are minimal as you'll notice people start trickling in about ten minutes before departure.

Off-hours and hideaways in hotels. After the maids have come through, and before the next round of guests check in, is an ideal time to get some peace in your hotel room, especially if it's anything but tranquil in the evening and early morning. The ideal time window is usually between noon and three p.m.

If you've already checked out of a hotel, don't feel bad about relaxing in the lobby a few hours after giving up your key. It's unlikely that any hotel employee will ask you to leave just because you're done and paid for; after all, they want you to come back on your next trip, and write a nice online review about your stay.

Finally, a surprising number of hotels – particularly in Europe – have rooftop terraces. These are often underutilized, because 1) guests aren't aware of them, or 2) they simply forget to head up there. The terrace can be a great escape when everyone else on your floor seems to be checking in, or coming in and out of their rooms, at the same time. An added benefit is that you get to see the city from a bird's-eye view, which can make it look less intimidating and give you a better perspective of where you are.

Airport quiet spots. For some peace and space, many people know to head to the waiting area of a deserted gate. Less commonly sought, but equally quiet places include interdenominational chapels (many international airports have one, and you don't have to pray in order to use the room), and the lobbies of pre-check-in areas. Most people automatically rush to the check-in counter and through security when they arrive at the airport, passing by many empty waiting areas adjacent to the airline ticket counters.

Travel Eating for Anxious People

Although it's not the only dining option on a trip, many people choose to eat at restaurants for convenience and to experience the local culture. Sources of stress while eating out can include:

- Social anxiety and uncertainty about making reservations, and interacting with waiters and waitresses;

- Excessive noise contributing to nervousness and loss of appetite;

- Worry about food safety;

- Self-consciousness about how you eat and handle utensils;

- Awkwardness about eating alone, if you're traveling solo; and

- Inability to choose from the typically vast number of restaurants available in a city.

Here are some guidelines for managing these sources of anxiety while eating out.

Ask for help with reservations. Dial up hotel reception staff from your room and tell them what type of place and food you're looking for, and how far away you're willing to go. Hotel staff know the best restaurants in the neighborhood since they often have to eat nearby themselves. Having them pick out and reserve a restaurant can make you feel more comfortable and taken care of, at least until you familiarize with the area.

Eat at off times. This translates as "early" in most countries. Try 11:30 for lunch, and 4:30 for dinner. Most restaurants open their doors at 11:00 in the morning, or just after. Eating at off times can be downright convenient if you haven't yet adjusted your hours to the local time.

Look for minimally staffed restaurants. It's easy to tell which restaurants are minimally staffed, or understaffed. Peek in the window or doorway and you'll see two or perhaps only one waitress (or waiter) rushing from table to table, managing too much food and too many people at once. While this is seen as a serious drawback by many, you might find it to have some definite advantages:

- The help is too busy to pay much attention to you, so you're less likely to feel self-conscious, put on the spot, or "watched";

- The other guests are too busy flagging the help down to notice you; and

- The help will take a while getting around to your table, allowing you more time to unwind and decompress before the meal.

Order warm food. If your nerves are raw and your stomach is twisted in knots, the last thing you want is a frigid salad or other cold dish. There's a reason that most "comfort foods" are warm or hot. Having some soup, or something out of the oven, will have a soothing effect on your central nervous system.

Sit close to the kitchen. You'll be too pleasantly distracted by all the different aromas to be affected much by other diners, and the chefs will have too much steam in their faces to notice you.

Suggestions for Those Who Have Had (or Have) an Eating Disorder

A disproportionate number of anxiety sufferers have experienced an eating disorder in their life, which – even if treated decades ago – can compound certain fears of eating out. These fears can include:

- Oversized portions that may lead to impulsive eating;
- Uncertainty about the number of calories in foreign dishes; and
- Inability to fully focus on or enjoy food unless alone.

Limited buffets, where you pay by the ounce instead of one all-you-can eat cost, can be ideal for addressing these fears since more food means more cost, yet you can choose what you want and what's familiar. It's fairly common to find these limited buffet dining options in large department stores abroad.

Another option is to try the food court at a local mall. You'll almost always find a recognizable chain such as Subway, McDonald's, or Pizza Hut here. While people love to knock "fast food," a number of items are nutritious and their familiar content and portion size might be of great comfort. And if you're traveling solo, you won't attract as much attention eating alone in the corner of a food court as in a booth at a restaurant.

The Advantages of "Deli Dining"

When you travel, you usually will not have a kitchen or kitchenette in your room or suite, and may feel that going "out" (whether to a restaurant, food court, or cafeteria) is your only option to eat. An alternative, however, is to buy some take-out food, or go to the nearest supermarket and find something from the deli to take back to your hotel. You could also take your food to a nearby garden, rooftop terrace, or other peaceful spot for a small picnic. This is a great way to "eat like a local" without going to a restaurant.

Additional advantages of eating from a market deli, or getting take-out, include:

- You come into contact with fewer people and their germs. You don't sit at a table which may not be fully sanitized, and you don't have to worry about plates or utensils that aren't well-washed;

- Your risk of food poisoning is greatly reduced since most deli and take-out foods are pre-cooked and moderately processed; and

- You eat when and where you want, instead of waiting for a restaurant to open and having to walk or ride there. In general, you have more control.

How to Sleep in a Noisy Place

People with anxiety disorders often suffer from sleep disturbances, even if medication side effects include drowsiness. Worrying about the amount and quality of sleep you get during your trip can be a significant mental hurdle. Just the fear of not getting enough sleep can make you anxious, since being tired can affect your judgment, stamina, and resilience, and make you more prone to getting ill.

You're probably well aware of common tips for drowning out noise, such as wearing earplugs, running a fan all night, or taking sleep medication so that you simply snooze through disruptions. There are times when these options may not be effective enough, available, or healthy. Here are some suggestions that don't involve toting along expensive and cumbersome noisemakers, or taking sedatives.

Television background noise. Setting your TV to a station receiving only static can give you just the right amount of background noise to help you fall asleep, and drown out sudden sounds from outside your room.

Move your bed around. There's nothing to stop you from moving your bed away from a window, or away from a door to a quieter part of the room. You might be surprised at what a difference even ten feet makes. If hallway noise is significant, then moving your bed under or near the window will help you tune more into the street noise (or lack thereof); conversely, if street noise is worse than hallway noise, then moving your bed closer to the room door can help you get some peace. And if you need help moving your bed, just ask the hotel staff; they're used to doing so to make space for rollaway beds or cribs.

Don't adjust to jetlag. At the start of your trip, you may want to sleep from about one to eight in the morning rather than the much earlier hours you keep at home. If the people on your floor are keeping the same hours as your "jetlag hours," you might consider not trying to adjust your times at all.

These three strategies should get you far in an average place of lodging with fairly responsible staff. If you find yourself rooming right next to an out-of-control party, or are on your own in an apartment rental with some very noisy people nearby, additional measures may be needed. Consider the following:

Don't confront people. Asking someone to "turn it down" is usually a waste of time and effort. People aren't deaf; they know they're being loud, and if they had the nerve to turn it up so loud, they probably have the nerve to ignore your plea for peace. Furthermore, 1) the rowdy crowd may pretend not to understand what language you're speaking; 2) you're likely to be greatly outnumbered; and 3) you're getting a full blast of hyper-stimulating party noise just by going over to confront someone. Perhaps worst of all, you may become anxious about being seen in the hallway for the rest of your trip once you've been stigmatized as "the complainer."

Ask for a different room. If accommodations staff won't do anything about the noise upstairs, then ask for a different room. If they can't or won't give you another room, then relax in the lobby. Chances are it's late and there will be few people checking in to disturb you.

I've actually dozed off in the lobby waiting for it to get quiet upstairs. Upon waking me up the receptionist was suddenly more than happy to find me a different, quiet room (which happened to be an upgrade to a suite).   Hotel staff were probably embarrassed to have an incoming guest see me curled up with a pillow and nodding off in their lobby. Whatever the case, I eventually got the peace and quiet I wanted.

Call code enforcement. In many budget hotels, staff will close the front desk for the night at about ten o'clock, leaving instructions for how to get in touch with them in the middle of the night if something comes up (including wild parties). You might find it quicker (and are certainly within your rights) to look up the local code enforcement in the white pages, and report the noise. All developed countries, and a good proportion of developing countries, have some sort of code officers who will respond to noise complaints.

If you're renting an apartment or house, then making the call yourself is usually a must. The landlord should leave you code enforcement numbers and other contacts before handing you the keys to the rental.

Transportation: Getting Around Without a Breakdown

As the old saying goes, *getting there is half the fun* so when you need to get moving, don't let your anxiety take you for a ride. In this chapter we'll look at the ups, downs, and roundabouts of every way you can get from "here" to "there." You'll see how understanding a bit about airplanes can help you find the most relaxing seat that you can afford. You'll learn how to avoid scrutiny of your medications while crossing international borders, as well as how to keep your pills safe while you're on the move. We'll look at the benefits and drawbacks of cruise vacations for anxiety sufferers, and you'll get a crash-course on how to confidently travel via intercity or long-distance train. We'll go over what you need to know about driving in a foreign country, and the benefits as well as the potential stress of touring on foot. I'll also share some navigational know-how to take the anxiety out of exploring on your own or with your companion.

Flying

Fear of flying is a widespread phobia among both anxiety sufferers and the general population. Since it's so prevalent, it may be safe to say that even though air travel was invented over one hundred years ago, it still feels unnatural to jet through the stratosphere at 500 miles per hour in a tube. I won't delve into the general fear of flying except to say that 1) planes undergo such rigorous safety checks, and have so many contingencies built into the flight that the chances of anything happening to you are slim to none, and 2) pilots want to land safely as much as you do, and will do everything in their power to do so. Even with this in mind, you usually have to build up a series of positive experiences on planes in order to overcome the fear of flying.

As someone with an anxiety disorder, the chances are you're just as worried about where you'll be sitting on the plane as you are about the flight itself. The usual anxiety triggers are:

1. Noisy seat neighbors, including children and babies;

2. Engine, bathroom, and kitchen noise; and

3. Comfort in your seat (i.e., people not kicking your seatback or invading your personal space).

Things that matter a lot to others, such as getting off the plane the fastest and getting served meals first, won't necessarily matter much to you. Whether you have a window, middle, or aisle seat will considerably affect your flying experience, but your overall stress level will also depend on 1) what, or who is in front and behind you, and 2) whether you're seated towards the front or back of the plane. While it's true that flying is a means to an end and that it's possible to spend too much time thinking about it, your seat comfort can seem like an eternity when you're one hour into an eleven-hour flight. If you arrive at your destination on the verge of an anxiety or panic attack, you might be looking a little too hard at the departures screen as you're collecting your bags, instead of looking forward to your vacation.

Choice of seat. Whether you've booked your ticket directly with an airline, or through a vendor such as Travelocity or Priceline, you have a right to contact the airline and put in a request for a certain type of seat. There's no guarantee that you'll get it, of course, especially if you've booked on short notice, but there's a good chance you'll get something close to what you want on at least one of the flights. You should describe your preferences (or undesirables) such as being seated near the kitchen; as far away as possible from the bathrooms; way in the back, etc., as well as simply asking the representative where the quietest seats are.

Here's what to know before you contact the airline.

Decreased stress with having no one seated in front of you:
1. No one will be leaning back on you to sleep
2. You're usually looking at a wall or a screen, which may help you forget that you're on a plane

Decreased stress with having no one behind you:
1. No one will be kicking the back of your seat, or stabbing the back of your headrest as they touch the in-flight entertainment screen
2. No one will be grasping your head rest to avoid stumbling down the aisle
3. You may be able to double-dip under-seat luggage space (both at your feet, and directly under your seat) if you feel more comfortable with all your things within immediate reach

Decreased stress with sitting towards the front of the plane:
1. Less motion sickness. As discussed in Chapter 2, severe motion sickness can contribute to an anxiety or panic attack

2. You'll be much closer to business class, which is almost always quieter

3. You'll be closer to the pilots, which might help you psychologically

Decreased stress with sitting towards the back of the plane:

1. You'll get a better feel for the size of the plane and who's in it, which you might find reassuring

2. The back of the aircraft is usually less crowded

3. You'll be much closer to the flight attendants, who can help with any number of questions or concerns

Decreased stress with aisle seats:

1. You won't have to ask people to get up so that you can use the lavatory

2. These seats are generally better for claustrophobia sufferers

Decreased stress with window seats:

1. Other passengers won't be staring at you as they make their way down the aisle

2. You'll be able to keep an eye outside, which may help you keep your bearings

One thing you should decide is whether you're willing to take a middle seat if it's in a quiet area of the plane. Middle seats are almost always the last seats chosen, but a quiet middle seat can more than make up for being wedged between two people. It also makes it more unlikely that you'll get two "talkers" next to you since on many planes (except the largest jumbo jets) you'll usually have one seat to your left and one to your right.

Here are some other things to consider on a flight.

Emergency exit rows. Many travelers ask for an emergency exit row seat because of the extra leg room, and don't think so much about the occupant's obligation to assist others in case of an evacuation. Do you think you would have the mental and emotional stamina to help others off the plane during an emergency? If not, then don't feel bad, and don't take a seat in an emergency exit row.

Different types of noise. There are basically two types of noise on a plane: human and non-human. The first includes screaming babies, small children, and rowdy or talkative passengers; the second includes the inevitable groaning, humming, slamming, or clattering from the bathrooms, the engines, or the kitchen. Understanding which of the two affects you more, and knowing where to expect each, can help you choose your seat accordingly.

The engines of commercial airplanes are most often located under the wings, or (less commonly) on the rear fuselage towards the tail. Some people seek out this noise because although it's very loud, it's consistent, making good background noise to drown out the occasional crash, slam, or bang. It's not unreasonable to ask an airline rep where the most engine noise is on a particular plane, and factor it into your decision.

Particularly on international flights, infants are typically placed in the first row of the coach section where hanging beds are available. Other places you're more likely to find babies and small children are closest to the restrooms (usually a convenience chosen by parents), which can be right in the middle of the plane in addition to the front and back.

Noisy seat neighbors are more difficult to predict. If there are unassigned seats on a full flight, you might try taking a middle seat in order to avoid two people finding seats next to you and chatting and laughing for the duration of the ride. If there are assigned seats on a

184

full flight and you find yourself in a rowdy area, ask a flight attendant if you can be reseated. Flight attendants receive at least a couple requests per flight for seat changes, for many reasons. You might happily trade your seat-back entertainment screen and noisy seat for someone whose entertainment screen is broken and who doesn't mind leaving a quiet area.

In Transit: How to Avoid Questions about Medications

The first time you really think about how many pills you're carrying around with you, and what they look like to someone else, is likely to be at the airport – specifically, in the passenger security line when leaving the country, and then the immigrations line wherever you land. It's no secret that practically every chemical compound ever manufactured by a pharmaceutical company has been abused, trafficked, or mishandled in some way or another, so the attention paid to your innocuous-looking supply can be understandable.

In general, you're allowed to land in a country carrying up to a one-month's supply of medications for personal use. Almost all countries have their own rules, however, about exactly what and how much you can enter with, and some of the rules are easier to understand than others. When being questioned about medications, you should have out your emergency medical card and attachments (as described in Chapter 5) including the signed letter from your psychiatrist describing your diagnosis and prescriptions. Here are some more specific guidelines for reducing the chance that your medications will be confiscated or that you'll be detained.

Compliance with INCB regulations. Two classes of medications, narcotics and psychotropics, are regulated under international law – specifically, by the International Narcotics Control Board (INCB) – because they have a significant effect on the Central Nervous System (CNS) and the potential to be abused. The narcotics class includes morphine and codeine, and generally isn't of much relevance to anxiety sufferers. Psychotropic drugs include just about every single medication used to treat anxiety disorders: SNRIs, SSRIs, benzodiazepines, and related families. The INCB website, located at www.incb.org, contains a number of statements and links regarding travel with psychotropics and narcotics; these are summarized below.

At the very least, you must have a letter from your doctor if you're traveling with a psychotropic or narcotic substance. The INCB requires countries to submit their own regulations regarding controls on medication; unfortunately, many have submitted incomplete or vague entries. Countries with the strictest laws include the United Arab Emirates, Russia, Australia, and Japan; other countries (particularly where some street drugs are legal, such as The Netherlands) have far fewer controls.

There is some inconsistency and confusion, both on the INCB website and beyond, in determining what exactly is prohibited, where. If you have a particular concern and your web research and phone calls prove futile, consider visiting the foreign country's nearest embassy before leaving on your trip, and request written documentation from an official.

Despite the confusion, and variation in rules around the world, there are few cases of travelers encountering serious problems when traveling with medications. Well over 50% of all travelers require some sort of medication, and customs officials in other countries have a trained eye for discerning normal use of medications from potential abuse and trafficking. The basic strategy to avoid questioning, confiscation, and delays is:

1. Be forthright;
2. Limit quantities;
3. Have plenty of documentation; and
4. Emphasize over and again that your medications are for personal use.

If you get stuck, ask the customs agent to call your psychiatrist, general care practitioner, or HMO.

Limited quantities. Many countries permit entry with only a 30-day supply of most medications. An impatient or distracted customs agent may see 90 pills in your bottle and demand to know why there are so many, until you explain that you need to take three per day. If he or she doesn't want to (or can't) read your prescription dose off the bottle, try pointing out the low potency of the medication.

There's a fine line between carrying a back-up supply of medications, and looking like you're carrying more than for your personal use. If you're questioned about carrying more pills than you will need, provide an explanation (such as that you are going on a river-rafting tour, and there's a chance that some of your pills could get damaged). The customs agent may demand to see a return airline ticket and a trip itinerary to ensure that you aren't landing in the country for the wrong reasons.

Original packaging. Any medications carried overseas should be left in their original containers and be clearly labeled. This is a requirement that's frequently overlooked by those who want to save room or use pillboxes. I was once detained by an Australian official because he didn't believe that my Prozac (which I'd poured into a small plastic bag with a piece of cotton) was actually Prozac. You can put your medications back in a pillbox after you've cleared customs.

Possible import license certificate requirements. Nations with particularly strict laws on entering with medications may require you to file for an import license certificate before landing with certain drugs – even in quantities for personal use. Go to (or ask your doctor to go to) http://usembassy.state.gov to access import license certificate requirements for various countries. A certificate, if required, usually involves fees and three or four pages of signed documentation. Medications from the SNRI, SSRI, and benzodiazepine classes of anti-anxiety drugs rarely make the list requiring a certificate, but laws can change quickly, so it's better to check.

Cruises

In addition to being one of the safest ways to travel, a cruise ship takes care of a lot of the travel logistics that might otherwise cause you a lot of anxiety. Cruises roll your transport, lodging, and dining services into one package, dropping you at the foot of beautiful places for shore excursions and giving you the feeling of a familiar refuge at the end of a day. For a small surcharge, cruise lines will also arrange your round-trip airfare to and from your home to the port(s) of call. Finally, booking a cruise ticket may be the only practical way to visit remote and unique destinations, such as Antarctica or the tiny island chains in the Indian and Pacific Oceans.

Here are several other things to consider when deciding whether or not to take a cruise.

Less privacy. Although many cruise floors are laid out similarly as the average resort hotel, the atmosphere is different from traditional "ground" lodging where everyone is often going their own way. Whether there are 200 or 2,000 people onboard, other passengers may regard you as their "fellow shipmate" and you're more likely to have people ask you to take their photo, make small talk in one of many public areas, and the like. You'll also have cabin stewards, attendants, and other staff (and there are a lot of staff aboard cruises!) greeting you at every turn. If you have social anxiety, these small but repetitive interactions could wear down your sense of privacy, and you may find yourself staying in your stateroom just to be left alone.

Confronting aggravations. There may be many things on a cruise that you'd normally avoid, such as bars, casinos, or all-you-can-eat buffets, because you've had a drinking or gambling problem, or an eating disorder in the past. The drawback of being on a ship for days is that you run into the same temptations over and over again, wearing down your resolve to stay away. Luckily, alcohol is rarely complimentary (everything else you can possibly consume is) so having to pay for something might be enough to keep you in control, but you should consider how you'll be affected by the carefree (or gluttonous, depending on how you look at it) attitude that comes with life on a cruise.

Claustrophobia. Despite the massive size of most modern cruise liners, people can feel confined and intensely claustrophobic without land around them. It may be hard to predict whether you'll suffer from this, even if you don't normally suffer from claustrophobia. The best option may be to start with a shorter cruise instead of a two- or three-week sailing, since claustrophobia on a ship tends to build gradually.

Medical facilities on board. If you decide to take a cruise, you won't be conducting the same search for emergency care abroad as you normally would. Instead, you should familiarize yourself with the medical services onboard. A cruise ship medical clinic isn't a floating hospital, but almost all have the capacity to provide emergency medical care for passengers and crew, stabilize patients for more serious conditions, and evacuate patients. It's very unlikely that there will be a psychiatrist on board, but the general care practitioner should be able to consult with you on psychiatric matters.

Understand that while many health-related issues are treated or managed onboard, shore-side consultation is not uncommon, particularly if you need a prescription filled (most cruise ships are unable to fill prescriptions onboard). The cost of such services could be significantly higher than if you pursued them independently in a port of call. The cruise doctor will direct (and often accompany) you to the recommended or appropriate shore-side care.

Prescription-strength motion sickness patches. People tend to experience motion sickness far more on ships than on planes, buses, or trains. If you are particularly susceptible to motion sickness, consider wearing a prescription-strength patch instead of relying on over-the-counter aids such as Dramamine. A popular and very effective prescription-strength motion sickness patch, Transderm Scop, is unfortunately known to cause drowsiness and dizziness in many individuals. You should discuss the side effects of any patches or motion sickness medications with your doctor, and make sure that there are no interactions with anti-anxiety medications.

Frequency of port stops. Days and days at sea can have an effect on people unlike no other. You may feel extremely vulnerable and overwhelmed floating on millions of gallons of water – even more than you might at seven miles high in an airplane. You may feel more at ease on a cruise with lots of port stops, that stays closer to land. The popular cruise routes down the Danube River in Europe, or from Seattle to Alaska, for example, will have more port stops than a cruise from Los Angeles to Hawaii. Because the ship keeps relatively close to the coastline, you're also more aware of where you are, which can reduce stressful feelings of disorientation and isolation.

Easing Anxiety on Trains

Most North Americans are largely unfamiliar with the nuances of train travel. Besides a possible Amtrak ride or two, you may have never had to navigate a station, look for train car and platform numbers, or try to figure out if a long-distance train stops in the small city you want to go to. Although train station attendants can assist you with these things, you'll be on your own to manage the psychological and physical stresses of train travel. This section will help you overcome these challenges so you can enjoy the scenery and unwind before you arrive at your next city.

Choice of seat. In almost all countries there are only two train classes: first class (including business class), and second class. There will usually be several more second-class cars on a train than first-class cars. It goes without saying that you'll find more peace and comfort in first class, but if money is an obstacle, you can still strategize to get the most relaxing seat possible in second class.

Most trains have a mix of booth seats and row seats. Booths seat two or three people on each side of a train compartment (which is typically about six feet long by six feet wide); compartments are separated from the car hallway by a glass door. A booth seat on a long journey, with two or three other strangers directly facing you (and possibly having nothing to do except watch you or talk to each other) is likely to cause you significant anxiety, even if you have a window seat and are trying to enjoy the scenery.

A row seat may be far more comfortable, since you'll probably prefer to look at the back of a seat instead of trying to avoid eye contact with several strangers. You should also have a decent view out the window, since row seats usually come in pairs on either side of an aisle; row seats also tend to be quieter, and offer more leg room. A train station attendant probably won't know if your incoming train has row seats or not, so you might stand at the far end of the platform and get a good look at each of the cars as the train pulls in to see where they might be.

Many long-distance trains require (or recommend) seat reservations, which can be made the same day of departure. If you're unhappy with the seat you've reserved, and you see an unreserved seat nearby, there's usually nothing to stop you from switching seats. If the area around your new seat gets noisy, you're entitled to return to your original seat for the duration of the ride (no one else has the right to take it even after you've left it).

Ventilation problems. Particularly in Asia and Latin America, trains can have poor air circulation, which can contribute to motion sickness, claustrophobia, and the ensuing anxiety. If you can't open any windows around you, then periodically stand between cars so that you can breathe fresh air pulled from outside. If you know in advance that ventilation will be a problem on the trains you take, try taking early morning trains when it's least likely to be stuffy and warm.

Dehydration. To a lesser (but still noticeable) extent than on planes, the recirculated air on trains can dehydrate you. Most trains have a dining car (usually located towards the center of the train) where you can purchase beverages, but be aware that these typically close down an hour (or even two hours) before the train reaches its final destination. You could find yourself stuck for quite a time towards the end of your ride without a few sips of water to swallow some pills. Don't resort to drinking from the lavatory sink as this water can make you ill.

Connections and delays. As with air travel, you can experience train travel delays either before or during your journey. Unlike with air travel delays, there's often no one to help you reschedule or compensate you should you miss your connection; you'll probably be told to find lodging within a couple blocks of the station (and there are usually plenty of places to stay) and come back the next morning to be on your way.

If this will wreak havoc on your plans, and the idea of walking around in the dark to find a nearby hotel terrifies you, try searching the station entry hall for the kiosks of privately-run trains. These will rarely be covered by rail passes but often fill in the gaps left by state-run trains, both in terms of availability and customer service. It's very likely that they run late at night; one of their main purposes is to board people who may otherwise be stranded. You'll have to pay a premium, but it might be a far more attractive option than staying overnight in an unfamiliar city.

Theft. Unfortunately, baggage theft comes with the territory of train travel. If you're traveling alone, and need to walk around or use the bathroom, you can 1) ask someone to watch your bags for you; 2) take a chance and leave your bags at your seat; 3) take your bags with you to the bathroom or down the hall with you; or 4) chain your luggage to the baggage rails over your seat. The last option will likely give you the most peace of mind without the stress of having to ask favors of anyone, stumble around the train with your bags, or come back to find that your belongings have disappeared.

Overnight trains. Also known as sleeper trains, these are generally not recommended for anxiety sufferers. What sounds like a good way to save some time and money will generally result in a sleepless and stressful night. Even in countries that lead the world in train travel, such as Germany and France, the conditions in sleeper cabins are uncomfortable, with no privacy and little room to move. Even in first-class booths, you may feel like you're stuck in a jail cell with a few strangers.

If you absolutely must travel overnight via train, take an intercity express night train, not a sleeper train. You'll have a standard upright seat just as you would on a day train, but most upright seats recline, so you should at least be able to take a nap. Intercity express night trains are almost always less crowded than sleeper trains, and they move faster, so you'll reach your destination by early morning instead of mid-morning.

Driving in a Foreign Country

While for many the idea of driving in a foreign country is an unsettling thought, some people with anxiety disorders have far more confidence in their navigational ability than in dealing with train schedules, ferries, buses, or hiring a taxi. Getting behind the wheel is a particularly attractive idea to those with social anxiety disorder. If you have a travel partner who can split driving time with you, then renting a vehicle abroad can be an even more appealing option.

Here are some other advantages to driving on your vacation:

- More time alone (or just with your travel partner);

- More flexibility since you're not bound to someone else's schedule;
- You get to see what you want, and *only* what you want, thereby lessening exposure to your anxiety triggers; and

- Less physical exhaustion since you won't be hauling luggage up and
  down train platforms, to and from bus stops, and the like.

There are a number of challenges to be aware of before you decide to rent and drive a vehicle abroad. Not all of them will apply in a given area, but understanding them can prevent some stressful encounters.

Sudden detours. I'm not talking about detours due to road construction, which are usually well-marked for drivers, but about streets and whole parts of a city cordoned off to accommodate an impromptu social or political protest, or poorly planned marathon or bicycle tour. To reduce your likelihood of running into one of these, ask the hotel receptionist upon check-out about the current local road conditions. There's no guarantee that they'll know about every possible detour or delay, but chances are they'll know more than you.

Road rage. It's not just an American phenomenon. Depending on what written or unwritten rules of the road you've violated, you may witness fists thrown out windows, shouting, prolonged honking, and various obscene gestures. Ask yourself some honest questions about how road rage impacts your anxiety, and find out more about the routes you plan to take. Long stretches of two-lane roads and hairpin-turn highways will inevitably lead to some sort of aggravation, either on your or someone else's behalf.

Tourists! Those annoyingly oblivious people on vacation who are jaywalking, blocking entrances to parking lots or attractions, and taking to the wheel themselves can elevate your anxiety through the roof of your rental car. The onus will usually be on you to make room for them and compensate for their mistakes.

Unwanted attention. As a foreign driver you can attract unwelcome attention either because your driving habits are different (not necessarily worse, and quite possibly *better* than the locals) or because your rental car has markings that identify it as such. It depends a lot on where you are, but you may be stared at by passing drivers, and you may develop an uncomfortable feeling of being followed.

Limited areas to pull over. In many cities, towns, and rural areas around the world, there is no shoulder on the side of the road – or the "shoulder" consists of a ditch or the bottom of someone's driveway. That means that if you do have a sudden anxiety or panic attack, you might have a hard time pulling safely off the road to recover.

Getting lost. Even if you have an excellent sense of direction, you may find it challenging to navigate where street names aren't posted, a series of one-way streets leaves your mind reeling, or the name of a single street changes every half mile (this is very common in historical city areas where too many aristocrats wanted their name bestowed on the main drag).

The Benefits and Drawbacks of Touring on Foot

There are relatively few places in the world where you can *only* tour on foot; even "pedestrian only" old towns and shopping districts in most regions are supplemented by trams, cable cars, and bicycle lanes. With that being said, walking is the only mode of transportation that is both free, and offers great freedom. Some of the advantages of enjoying your trip at two, three, or four miles per hour include:

- Any kind of exercise helps you manage anxiety by loosening your muscles and easing body tension;

- Moving at a slower pace means you have more time to absorb and appreciate the scenery than you would at thirty, fifty, or eighty miles an hour;

- You'll have a great sense of empowerment from making it to a beautiful place or attraction on your own two legs; and

- You control yourself and where you go. There are few things that will make you feel more helpless abroad than boarding the wrong bus or train and having it take you blocks or miles out of your way before you can get off, figure out where you are, and start over.

Here are some of the drawbacks of getting around on foot:

- Instead of being surrounded by the same group of people on the metro or bus, you're passing a steady stream of strangers, some of whom may make you feel anxious and intimidated;

- There's a higher chance of mild or moderate accidents and injuries such as slipping, tripping, and falling. In order to avoid a more serious injury, you'll also need to recognize and heed bike lanes, particularly where they are poorly marked;

- You'll need to keep a wary eye out for drivers turning on your green light, as well as drivers who don't respect traffic signals at all. (You can generally find out more about a city or country's driving habits and accident rates by consulting the average tour book);

- Getting lost can be an exhausting and painful experience, even when you're only off by a few blocks. If you know an area is going to be confusing, try getting a ride there the first time, and then walking there after that. Another strategy is to plan confusing or remote areas of town for earlier in the day when you have more energy, and more familiar and accessible areas for later (where you're more likely to find a bus or taxi back if you really need one).

As mentioned in the last chapter, you should not assume that sidewalks and walking paths exist wherever you want to go. Popular tourist destinations such as Canada, Australia, and New Zealand can suffer from a significant lack of sidewalks; in many cases, pedestrian access in developing countries is much better (mainly because the average person can't afford a car!).

Finally, you should beware of frustrating walking conditions in areas predominated by canals, rivers, and small lakes. Bridges can be few and far between, and you might spend a lot of time and energy backtracking to get where you need to go. Compounding the problem is that these areas are notoriously flat, so you might not see your destination until you're practically on top of it.

Essential Navigation Tips

Even the best intentions to build modern cities on a grid have often been thwarted by the shape of a coastline, the river around which a city grew, or a mountain range that creates impasses and geological challenges to laying asphalt. All sorts of other things – from rail stations to landfills to poorly sited stadiums to ancient ruins – can make a city twist and turn like a labyrinth instead of welcoming you with neat parallels and perpendiculars.

Getting lost in an urban maze when you're already tired, dehydrated, or hungry, with the sun setting and not a taxi in sight, can severely overwhelm you and lead to an anxiety attack. Fear of losing one's way is often cited by tourists as a main reason for choosing a group tour. If you're traveling with a tour, the only time you need to worry about getting lost is when you have to rejoin the group. If you're traveling alone or with someone who has a poor sense of direction (i.e., is relying on you) then you'll benefit from understanding the following.

Don't automatically rely on the sun for direction. If you're at similar latitudes as your home city, or if you're vacationing near the equator, then you should have no trouble equating the sunrise with east and the sunset with west. However, at far latitudes both north and south, the sun makes more of an ellipsis across the sky, so what looks like the sun setting in the west is actually more northwest or southwest, and what looks like the sun rising in the east is actually more northeast or southeast.

Another problem is that you simply won't be able to see the sun in skyscraper districts of large cities; unless it's almost directly overhead, it will be blocked from view by the buildings.

Finally, some of the most charming and exasperating places to get lost are in Northern Europe, where the sun doesn't come out at all on many days.

Rivers. Almost every major city in the world is built around or on a river, a lake, a sea, or an ocean. Of the four waterways, rivers are the least reliable for helping you navigate since they tend to be anything but straight, and often join another river flowing from an adjacent direction. "Follow the river" and you could end up making a perfect *C*-shape around a city, without the foggiest idea of how to get back to your hotel.

Inner-city islands. Many cities, particularly in Europe, have small islands in the center of wide-mouthed rivers (either by nature or by design) and can make tempting landmarks. Unfortunately, "river islands" tend to be so inconspicuous that you can walk on or off one without even noticing. Bridges supported entirely by beams are difficult to spot from any direction since they're very low to the water. If your hotel is on a river island and you're coming back in the dark, pick an overhead landmark so you don't walk right on and right off your island.

Compasses. These may seem like a no-brainer convenience to help you start out and stay headed in the right direction. The problem with compasses is that they don't allow you to react to your environment. What good is a compass if it tells you to head north, but the first few steps that direction is down a dead-end street leading to the city's sewer treatment system? You might need to head east, and then northwest, and *then* north in order to get where you need to go.

If you're in a confusing area, and only have a map, there's sometimes no easy solution for staying on track except to double-check street names on a map before taking each new turn.

Surrounding coastline. It may be tempting to rely on coastline as a reference point for maneuvering a city. However, many coastal cities are situated on peninsulas, with coastline on three of four sides. When you see water, what you're convinced is south may actually be east or west. Unless there are some defining landmarks on each coast (such as a lighthouse or public beach), relying on the coastline to steer you home can lead to frustration and stress.

Landmarks. I once picked a sparkly green billboard in London as my landmark to walk back to the King's Cross Tube station, only to realize on the way back (after going a mile out of my way) that the billboard was not only one-sided, but completely obscured from the rear by construction machinery. If you're going to use landmarks to guide you, learn from my mistake and pick those that are three-dimensional and high enough to not be blocked from view from any direction.

Metro stations can make great landmarks since they both 1) show up on a map, and 2) are well-marked on the streets. Just be aware that most stations have entrances on either side of the street, and sometimes two (or even more) entrances on both sides. You'll want to reference the street corner closest to the entrance you picked to avoid confusion.

Finally, see Chapter 10 for information on how augmented reality navigation applications can guide you through a city.

How to Keep Your Pills Safe While You're on the Move

With all this talk about getting around, it's worth discussing how to safeguard some of your most precious cargo: your medications. As you probably know, pharmaceutical manufacturers recommend that most medications be stored between 68 and 77 degrees Fahrenheit. Realistically, anywhere from 58 to 86 degrees should be no problem; just check the bottle, or with your pharmacist to make sure. Above or below this range, pills can physically or chemically change, resulting in lost potency, degradation into another compound that could affect your liver or kidneys, or separation and reconstitution that could result in an overdose (or no dose) if you are splitting pills.

Typical precautionary measures include keeping pills in their original packaging, avoiding exposure to the sun, keeping bottles out of humid environments (including bathrooms), and storing pills indoors with you as much as possible. Here's some other essential guidance.

Recognizing damaged pills. Never take any medications that have changed color or consistency, have an unusual odor, are sticking together, or are harder or softer than normal. Pay more attention than you normally would to your pills before and while swallowing them.

✗ You should *not* throw away damaged medications; instead, take them to the local pharmacy when asking for (and justifying) replacements. The next chapter will discuss in more detail how to get medications replaced at a pharmacy.

Prevent hotel theft. Unfortunately, your pills – as psychotropic drugs – often rank above petty cash in their attraction to unscrupulous maids. It's unlikely that your whole bottle will be stolen, but enough pills may be taken to cause you to run short towards the end of your trip. Before you leave your room for the day, put your pill bottle in your suitcase, and lock your suitcase.

Too cold is better than too hot. Heat is generally more likely to induce a physical or chemical change in a medication. If you're forced to choose between temperature extremes, go for the cold (such as storing a bottle in an ice cooler on a hot day's hike, rather than in your pocket).

Beware of baggage holds. Always carry your medications onto the plane, even if it means more headaches at security checkpoints. Baggage holds are not always controlled for temperature and can easily drop below 40 degrees, or soar above 90 degrees.

Pack extra cotton. Take extra cotton balls on your trip since they rarely make the "in case you forget" list of complimentary hotel amenities, and can be surprisingly hard to find in pharmacies abroad.

CHAPTER 8

Avoiding, Managing, and Recovering from Psychiatric Emergencies

Throughout this book we've focused on how to manage anxiety, and how to prevent an anxiety or panic attack. If you do have an attack during your trip, there are many steps you can take to make it less traumatic, as well as prevent misunderstandings or improper triage while you are seeking help. In the following pages you'll learn who is in a position to assist you in the event of a psychiatric emergency, and to what extent. We'll go over what to do if your medication runs out on your trip, as well as how to recognize counterfeit medications you may be offered. Finally, you'll understand how to manage yourself in a medical clinic or hospital abroad, and how you can recover in a foreign environment to enjoy the rest of your trip.

Tour Until You Drop?: Warning Signs That You've Had "Enough"

If you've physically and mentally prepared for your trip, you should be able to see, do, and enjoy more in a single day than you would during a typical weekend at home. If you're well into a hectic but rewarding trip and start to feel yourself suddenly wearing down, then you'll need to take steps to protect your mental and emotional well-being. You've undoubtedly discussed your thresholds for stress and stimulation with your psychiatrist before, and how to tell when to scale back – even when you're in a completely different environment. Of course, it's one thing to understand your personal limits; it's another to respect them, or pay attention to how you're really feeling when you're surrounded by distractions. The following are some serious signs that you're approaching your mental and emotional limits as a traveler, and need to take it easy as soon as possible.

- Other people (such as your tour guide or hotel receptionist) notice and ask about physical signs of stress you display, such as trembling, pallor, or sweating;

- You're unable to make basic decisions, such as whether to take your jacket with you before you leave your hotel room;

- You can't remember what you saw or where you were two hours ago – or fifteen minutes ago;

- Your physical, mental, and emotional states are not in harmony. For example, you feel hyper, invincible, or restless, but at the same time ready to crumble, cry, or collapse;

- You commit serious mistakes, such as unintentionally walking on a red light, or leaving a store with unpaid merchandise; or

- You're growing increasingly impatient with the people of your host country and are now doing things "your way," accompanied by feelings of anger and frustration.

If you experience any of these, regroup by practicing some of the techniques you use if you've just had an attack: lie down in a quiet area, close your eyes and put in earplugs, focus on your breathing, and the like. If you're not traveling solo, try to be as communicative as possible with your companion about what you're going through, and whether you need to be left alone for a while or not.

Self-Assessment: **Acknowledging Your Personal Limits**

What trip activities do you think could lead you to exhaust or overwhelm yourself?

_____

_____

_____

_____

What's standing in the way of reassessing your original plans and changing them?

_____

_____

_____

_____

Who and what would be affected if you don't make a particular excursion, activity, or travel goal?

_____

_____

_____

Who Can (and Will) Help You During an Anxiety or Panic Attack?

In Chapter 4 we looked at how cultural perceptions of mental illness can impact a person's response to you as an anxiety sufferer. This section focuses on interacting with strangers in various roles – particularly different types of service people – if you start to experience or display symptoms of an anxiety or panic attack. These people may call for help, assist you in finding and taking pills, help you practice taking deep breaths, keep you warm or cool, ensure that you can rest safely, and may even keep away individuals who take advantage of people who become ill.

Beyond the cultural and social factors discussed in Chapter 4, the extent to which a stranger may assist you usually depends on:

- Safety concerns and the individual's responsibility for the well-being of others;

- Your perceived physical stability or infectiousness;

- Your appearance and level of calmness;

- Your status as a paid or unpaid guest; and

- If, and how well, you're able to communicate during an anxiety or panic attack.

The majority of attack symptoms do not resemble those of alcoholism or drug addiction, so you're unlikely to receive an indifferent or hostile response from someone who witnesses your distress. Many people have gotten seriously ill in public before – such as from food poisoning or the flu – and are likely to be sympathetic, or at the least will get out of your way. However, keep in mind that:

- Symptoms such as unsteadiness and shaking are usually

perceived as a threat to merchandise, public property, or exhibits; and

• Attack responses such as sudden lunging, squatting, or seizing could be perceived as a physical threat, particularly to children or the disabled.

If you are traveling alone, or will be separated from your travel companion at any time during your trip, recognize that you may have to rely on understanding service people to get you the help you need during an anxiety or panic attack. You should also understand that for a variety of reasons – including access, awareness, and concerns about liability – they are better to assist you than other tourists, or local citizens. Understand the following about various types of service people.

Hotel staff. Probably the best place to be if you're having an attack is your "home" in a foreign country – either your hotel room, or the hotel lobby. Most hotel personnel have some training in first aid or experience in helping sick or injured people, and if they don't, they will try to make you comfortable until you decide whether to seek medical help to bring your attack under control. They're also likely to assist you by finding the nearest urgent care (if you don't have the information) or by calling a taxi.

Restaurant staff. Since people regularly see each other off, propose, or break up over meals, most waiters and waitresses are used to seeing people in distress or overly emotional. If your symptoms or gestures are more physical (such as gasping for air, excessive sweating, holding your face, etc.), understand that their first inclination is to assume a food allergy. Therefore, if you are approached by restaurant staff, you should state that you do not have an allergy (and if you can talk, then they understand that you can't be choking) and allow them to dial help for you.

Store clerks. Staff of larger stores, rather than smaller stores, will be more able and willing to assist you during an attack. Small shops have only one or two employees who may struggle to maintain control of their business if they attempt to help you.

If you're in any position to damage sensitive merchandise, let the clerk steer you to another area (such as an employee lounge) or immediately outside the store, and dial a taxi or ambulance for you.

Taxi drivers. Yes, they have a universal reputation for being gruff, impatient, and generally unhelpful. However, we've discussed how ambulance services don't exist in many developing countries (or you may not be in a position to dial one) so taxis are your next best option for prompt transport to medical help. If you find yourself needing one during an attack, pre-pay (and overpay) the driver and explain that you have a preexisting medical condition, and need the closest medical clinic or hospital. Don't just say that you are ill, because the driver will assume that you'll leave a trail of vomit or blood in his cab. Try to sit up, and let the driver focus on getting you to the nearest medical care as quickly as possible.

Bus drivers. Since they are actively steering a vehicle, and are usually on a tight schedule, bus drivers are unlikely to be able to help you. Even at a stop, they could dangerously impede traffic by trying to assist you. Also, keep in mind that bus drivers come in more frequent contact with alcoholics and drug addicts than others in the service and transportation sectors, and may be wary of having anything to do with someone whose exact cause of distress is unknown.

Use your judgment regarding whether it's better to stay on the bus or not. If you are far away from your scheduled stop, ask another passenger if the bus passes a hospital or medical clinic. It's inadvisable to get off at the first stop after the onset of an anxiety or panic attack unless you're familiar with the area.

Train attendants and ticket inspectors. Unlike bus drivers, these individuals have their hands free and are in a better position to help you. While first class cars and more expensive trains have attendants who work just to ensure your comfort and safety, second class attendants are harder to come by, and the ticket inspector could be more interested in seeing your ticket first and may then call another inspector or attendant from a nearby car to help you. Communicate as best as possible that your symptoms are not the result of motion sickness, or the flu or another communicable illness. Train staff will likely advise you to get off at the next medium- to large-sized station, and will radio someone there to assist you in finding an ambulance, taxi, or hospital.

Finally, be aware that train attendants and ticket inspectors are largely a European and North American phenomenon. Asian and Australasian countries, in particular, are unlikely to have inspectors or attendants on board, except for attendants in dining car(s). The metro in most countries is also very unlikely to have onboard attendants, so get off at the nearest station and consult staff at the kiosk or exit.

Under no circumstances should you try to communicate with the train conductor unless you are parked at an end-of-the-line station.

Stewards/stewardesses. If you feel an anxiety or panic attack coming on during a flight, notify the flight attendant as soon as possible, and (given the lack of space around any given seat) be prepared for them to help you to the back of the plane. Try to remember to take your medications with you. The flight attendant will closely monitor and inquire about your condition since every attendant's nightmare is to have to recommend an emergency landing to the pilot because of an onboard medical problem.

You should clarify that you have a preexisting medical condition and that your anxiety or panic attack is not an overreaction to fear of flying. The flight attendant will usually solicit a doctor or nurse on board. On larger planes an attendant may help you to the employee sleeping quarters, or to the upper level, so that you can lie down and regain control of your symptoms.

Police/peace officers. In most places police do far more than keep the peace, and they may be instrumental in finding you help. Don't be intimidated to ask for assistance since most peace officers welcome a chance to assist instead of detain, interrogate, or arrest someone (and for better or worse, many view getting sick or injured people off the streets as part of keeping the peace). Depending on where you are, the police may have the authority to expedite arrival of an ambulance, or order a taxi driver to take you to a clinic or hospital.

GOOD SAMARITAN LAWS

At this point you're probably wondering if Good Samaritan laws exist in other countries for assisting ill and injured people. Good

Samaritan laws offer legal protection to people who give reasonable, consensual assistance to those who are injured, ill, in peril, or otherwise incapacitated. The protection is meant to reduce a bystander's reluctance to assist a stranger (for fear of being sued or prosecuted for unintentional injury or wrongful death). Good Samaritan laws are prevalent in the United States, Canada, and Australia, and far less common elsewhere.

A principle of "duty to rescue" applies as law in many European countries. Duty to rescue typically criminalizes failure to help someone who is in critical danger, unless doing so would put the bystander at significant risk themselves. This means that you might get help in these countries because people are afraid *not* to help you (and it doesn't matter if you're a foreigner, or not). This could be reassuring to you, but you should be aware that someone getting you out of harm's way may not have any information or ability to get you to the nearest clinic, doctor, or hospital, and is not obliged to stay and help you once you're in a safer area.

Since Good Samaritan and duty to rescue laws primarily exist in developed nations, does that mean that you're on your own if you're in a developing country? Not necessarily. There are various social, moral, or religious influences in dozens of cultures that will encourage passersby to help someone who is clearly ill or in danger. Obligations to guests (including tourists) are very highly regarded in many countries, and the need to maintain public order also motivates strangers to assist others.

What to Do if You Have a Psychiatric Emergency Abroad
In general, you need to do the following if you have an anxiety or panic attack:

1. Get off your feet;

2. Find a quiet place to rest, and preferably lie down;

3. Take medication; and

4. See a doctor to bring symptoms and manifestations under control, discuss any new or unusual symptoms, identify additional medications that may be needed, and rule out a serious medical condition.

You inherently know that you need to do these things; what will present a challenge during an attack abroad is managing your unfamiliar surroundings, and interacting with strangers. If you have an attack during your vacation, the chances are it will be in public, since – realistically – this is where you encounter the majority of anxiety triggers. Although it's uncomfortable to think about, you'll need to be prepared to bring your attack under control as quickly as possible; prevent being misunderstood or taken advantage of by the people around you; and understand where you're being taken, if anywhere, for medical assistance. You'll need to be capable of all this when you're feeling (to put it bluntly) violently ill, so mental preparation is essential. Here's what you need to know.

Belongings. Keep control of your purse or wallet, medical insurance card, hotel information, and passport at all times. If you are so ill that you're unable to manage all these items, hold onto your passport and medical information and ask your tour guide, service staff, local authority, or (as a last resort) a stranger to manage your other belongings for you. Of course, there's no guarantee that they can and will do this, but it's better than expecting your valuables to automatically follow you wherever you go, or be where you left them hours or days later.

Confusion with other conditions or illnesses. We reviewed the typical symptoms of anxiety disorders in Chapter 2. Unfortunately, bystanders can interpret many of these symptoms – including shortness of breath, unsteadiness, excessive sweating, uncontrollable shaking, weakness, pallor, and disorientation – as signs of a physical medical condition that they're more familiar with. There is therefore the possibility that your manifestations will be mistaken for cardiac arrest, asthma, food poisoning, shock from injury, diabetes, severe flu, hyperventilation, epilepsy, pulmonary embolism, or many others.

Given the range of these possible assessments, and the potential for someone to triage you for the wrong kind of treatment, you should be prepared to clarify the reason for your symptoms – to the extent that it won't trigger stigma that will impede your care. The best way may be to explain that you have a *preexisting physiological medical condition.* This will help people rule out the possibilities above, while still assisting you in getting urgent care.

If no one seems to understand what a preexisting physiological medical condition is, then state the significant symptom or consequence of your condition *that is the most widely recognized.* In most cases, the best thing to say is that you may faint (which could very well be the case if you feel lightheaded, dizzy, or are suffering blackouts). This is much more easily understood than anything you could explain about a panic or anxiety attack.

Remember, you don't have to answer questions about your disorder, or yourself, if you think it will result in you 1) being taken to a mental hospital or institution; 2) being taken advantage of; or 3) result in any action that will worsen your condition or compromise your safety.

Visual signs of distress. If you are coping with a significant language barrier, you may have to resort to gestures to communicate what you need and what you're feeling. A universal sign that you are weak-legged and might pass out is to put your hands to your eyes, or close your eyes and put your hand to your forehead. This will at least encourage others to help you get off your feet, and find a quiet place to rest.

Be aware that some of your distress signals could be misinterpreted. Consider:

- If you hold the back of your head, people may think you have suffered a fall, which could be counterproductive to you taking medications and talking to a psychiatrist.

- If you hold your chest, people may think you are having a respiratory emergency.

- If you hold your stomach, people could suspect that you have the flu or food poisoning, and may be confused or try to intervene when you try to take your medication.

- If you hold your neck, people may believe you are choking or have a neck injury.

If you're already sitting or lying down, then try to keep your hands on your belongings, and off your body.

Understanding perceptions of disturbing the peace. Panic and anxiety attacks often come with symptoms that can look frightening or even threatening, such as lunging, trembling, stumbling, or bolting. You could stop suddenly in the middle of a busy thoroughfare, blocking people from going by, or cry or yell in a manner that alarms others. Different cultures have different ideas about what constitutes disturbing the peace, and making a scene. What could be called a disturbance of the peace in the ultra-orderly streets of Singapore, for example, is barely going to raise heads nine hundred miles away in the chaotic streets of Bangkok.

Although manifestations of anxiety and panic attacks are often difficult to control, you should use your understanding of a culture's tolerance for mental health problems, and its tolerance for personal expression, to protect yourself from being mistreated during a psychiatric emergency. Such mistreatment can include:

• Grabbing or handling you roughly;
• Verbal abuse including belittling, swearing, and yelling;
• Denied entry onto a bus or train; or
• Being asked to leave a restaurant or tourist attraction.

The best way to avoid this kind of treatment, besides understanding cultural factors, is to 1) react slowly to your surroundings, and 2) stay as quiet as you can. If you suffer from severe shaking or involuntary movements, stop walking as soon as possible; find the nearest chair or acceptable place to sit down. Cultures that don't appreciate yelling or crying in public are often much more attuned to other signs of distress, so if you need help, it won't be long before someone observes your physical state, and (if you're unable to help yourself) either offers to help you, or finds someone who can. If you are able to help yourself, or it appears that you're waiting for a travel companion to come back for you, then people will generally leave you alone, since there's no reason to believe that you're a threat to anyone.

Language barriers. We talked in Chapter 6 about the most straightforward ways to manage language barriers abroad. During a panic or anxiety attack, the three things you will specifically need to communicate to strangers are:

1. *I need a place to rest;*

2. *I need to take my medication;* and

3. *I need a doctor.*

The average travel language phrase-book contains these short sentences; if yours doesn't, then you'll be able to piece them together using the mini-dictionary in the back of your phrase book.

Triage. There are few things that will aggravate a panic or anxiety attack more than being in a foreign country and not knowing where you are being taken. You should make every attempt to communicate where you want to go, even if you worsen your symptoms in the process. Read off or point to the clinic or hospital listed on your emergency medical card; if the people helping you don't know where it is, call an ambulance. If there are no ambulance services, ask someone to dial a taxi, and give the driver the address of the hospital or clinic.

Documents. When you arrive at a clinic or hospital, your emergency medical card and supplements should be the first thing you present, or have presented for you, since they will expedite your treatment. Your documents should preferably be in a bright plastic folder or sealed, damage-resistant bag.

Remember that presenting your documents isn't the same as handing them over. A responsible medical receptionist will make copies of needed documents, or place them in the filer on your room door – not walk off with them. If you feel that you've entered a clinic or hospital where protocols are lax, ask the person or people with you to help keep track of your documents for you.

Treatment and Recovery

We've discussed that in most instances and countries, it's in your best interest to be treated at a general care hospital or clinic and not at a mental health clinic or institution. The last thing you want is to be committed, because you lose control over your own care, including the ability to leave the hospital. Even if it means losing track of your personal belongings or costing you a lot of money, you need to keep your bearings well enough to communicate, or have someone else communicate, the plan of treatment you've discussed with your doctor at home.

Generally you are committed when you are (or are perceived to be) unable to care for yourself, or a threat to yourself or others. You can mitigate someone's intention to have you committed by:

1. Remaining calm;

2. Responding to basic questions; and

3. Staying conscious and aware of your surroundings, even if it makes you feel sicker to do so.

Upon checking in (or being checked in to) a hospital, ensure that the hospital will release you on your own, or at the very least to your PTC or travel companion. You should establish early on with the attendant doctor that you have prescribed medications for an anxiety disorder; you should also make sure that they review your emergency medical card and supplemental documents. Once they do this, allow them to conduct a general physical exam. The latter is necessary to 1) ensure that you didn't unknowingly injure yourself (such as cutting your knee during a fall) during the attack, and 2) to rule out a sudden-onset physical illness. There are some rare but serious cases where people with an anxiety disorder have insisted that they were having a panic or anxiety attack, but in fact were suffering from cardiac arrest, toxic shock syndrome, or another life-threatening physical problem.

Once you've been cleared of injuries or sudden illness, it's possible that your attending physician will prescribe sedatives to take in addition to your normal medication. You should have the doctor write down specific instructions and side effects for the new medication(s), beyond what is typed on the bottle; don't take for granted that the medication will come with an informational page, or that you'll be able to remember everything the doctor tells you. If possible, have the doctor fax or email your psychiatrist information about the newly prescribed medication, as well as documentation of your admission and pending release.

Once you're released from the hospital, you need to decide whether, and how fast, you can resume your trip. Here are some important things to consider when determining whether or not to return home or push on.

Amount of recovery time needed. How long it will take you to recover from a panic or anxiety attack can have a significant impact on downstream travel plans, particularly if you've booked a series of one-way flights or train rides. It may be several days before you're able to even listen to street noise or engage with strangers without heart palpitations, profuse sweating, and other manifestations. You'll also need to identify whether you'll be in stressful or intense situations in the coming days that could lead to a relapse.

Some signs that you're not recovering well are 1) your medication doesn't feel like "enough" to be taking, and 2) you can't remember what you were doing in the days leading up to your anxiety or panic attack.

Impact on group. Some smaller tour groups can't, or won't, move forward without all members. If you're in limbo about continuing your vacation, you could be holding up other people. Talk to your tour guide about how you could possibly catch up with your group by flying to the next excursion while the rest of the group takes the bus. For adventure tours, it may be particularly difficult to pick up where you left off.

Don't feel awkward or embarrassed when talking to a tour guide about these things; they are used to people having to scratch or rejoin a tour, for any number of reasons. If it still causes you too much stress to talk to the tour guide, ask your travel companion or psychiatrist to do so for you.

Further insurance coverage. Many, if not most, insurance policies will only cover initial treatment, and expect you to return to your source of primary care once you've stabilized. Don't make assumptions about continual treatment abroad that could be financially devastating. Call or send an urgent email to your provider to obtain the facts.

Ability to fly. You need to be in a fairly good mental state to handle flying, even if you have someone escorting you to the airport and packing and checking your luggage for you. Consider whether you'll be able to deal with potentially long lines and loud crowds, and be able to keep track of your carry-on bag. Consider, also, how long the flight home is, and how many layovers you have. If you are booking a sudden ticket home, you might have to deal with more layovers than normal since direct flights may not be available on short notice.

Effect on confidence. Returning home is undoubtedly a difficult decision that could not only affect your confidence, but (particularly if you're traveling alone) your loved ones' confidence in your ability to travel safely and successfully in the future. If you are someone whose confidence depends on a series of successes, consider that scratching the rest of your trip – rather than trying to salvage it – will be a large step back. You should also understand that while going home will be more comfortable, it will not necessarily "take care of everything." Significant feelings of regret and loss could cause you stress, and you should consider how aborting your trip will impact your anxiety levels before or during the next trip you take.

If you assess your recovery, your plans, and your emotional state and decide to continue your trip, consider the following.

Identify and address triggers. It will be uncomfortable to relive the onset of your anxiety or panic attack, but go back to that moment and identify what exactly was responsible. Was it a buildup of many stressful experiences, or a single incident? The latter will be easier to address. For example, if you had an attack after a near-miss such as a bicyclist or car almost hitting you, consider how unlikely it is that such a thing will happen again, and what you can do to improve your safety. If you had an attack after going to a museum that stirred many painful memories or feelings, is it safe to assume that you won't experience the same feelings if you simply don't return to that place?

Tour the easy way. If a buildup of many stressful experiences led to your attack, then scale back and change how you tour. If you were walking and taking overcrowded metros to chaotic tourist sites full of stresses such as pickpockets, aggressive panhandlers, groping drunks, potholes, and suicidal motorcyclists, consider buying a 24-hour pass on a "hop-on, hop-off" sightseeing bus that breezes past, idles, or stops at the best and most popular sites. You will expend far less personal effort than you normally would to see many of the same things, and you don't have to get off the bus at all unless you want to. Other advantages include being able to breathe fresh air on the open-air bus, and ending up right back where you started (preferably, your comfortable hotel). There are "hop-on, hop-off" buses run by several companies in over 200 cities around the world.

Seek a restful environment. You might consider moving into the countryside for the remainder of your trip, or for the duration of your recovery period. For example, if you had a panic attack while staying and touring in downtown London and need several days to get back to normal, book at a B&B twenty miles away and rest there until you leave London for Amsterdam at the end of the week.

What to Do and Where to Go If Your Medication Runs Out

During a trip, you could run out of medications for a number of reasons: theft, confiscation, damage, loss, or simply having the bad luck of dropping the contents of your bottle down the drain of your hotel bathroom. Also, if you're taking a certain medication on an as-needed basis, you may find halfway through your trip that you didn't pack enough to last you through, and need to get some more. This section goes over how to get what you need so you don't risk sudden withdrawal, and going untreated.

Shipping medications to yourself. If you plan to have a family member or doctor ship medications to you while you're abroad, make sure that the laws of your destination country allow this by checking the U.S. Embassy's country-specific listings at http://travel.state.gov/travel/cis_pa_tw/cis/cis_4965.html#F. If there are no listed restrictions, then have the person at home label the parcel as medication, and insulate the bottle for protection from extreme temperatures and humidity. The parcel will need to be delivered from a main post office, and may be subject to delays including 1) time for security officials to screen it and possibly open it, and 2) time for regulatory agencies, both in your home country and destination country, to screen it. The truth is, your medications may have a harder time getting to your destination on their own than they would with you.

Theft is another concern. Your labeled parcel of psychotropic medication will have to go through a variety of hands – customs staff, delivery men, and hotel personnel – before they make it to you. Any unscrupulousness in the chain could result in the entire parcel disappearing. Since the countries with reliably safe post are usually the same ones where you can locally obtain the medications you need, shipping medications to yourself might be a moot point in some cases.

Local purchase. If you're in a part of a developing country where you haven't researched pharmacies, but you see one nearby, call your psychiatrist with its location and have them verify its license and authenticity. There are many small markets and street vendors abroad masquerading as legitimate pharmacies. If it looks too easy to get pills, then stay away; a telltale sign is a "pharmacist" who isn't reviewing or requesting prescriptions.

Honoring prescriptions. Once you've found a legitimate pharmacy, show the attending pharmacist or physician a copy of your original prescription, and signed letter from your doctor, to facilitate the consultation. Prescriptions written in the United States or Canada may not be automatically filled overseas. The attending pharmacist may have additional questions about the origin of the prescription, and about your doctor. Provide additional documentation or information as required, such as your doctor's medical license number; if you don't have the information, ask the pharmacist or attending doctor to call or email your psychiatrist. Be patient; they may be used to scams, and are only trying to protect their liability.

Unavailability. Be aware that some medications will not be available in your host country (for various reasons, including contracts with local pharmaceutical companies). An attending pharmacist or doctor may offer you a close alternative instead. Do not overreact or automatically suspect that you're being offered a counterfeit; a slight change in an inactive ingredient could be the only difference between your usual medication and the alternative. Ask to use the pharmacist's phone to talk to your own psychiatrist about the alternative – or have your psychiatrist discuss directly with the pharmacist.

Different dosages. The same medication offered in another country may not come in exactly the same dosage and potency that you require or are used to. Instead of the usual 400 mg tablets you take twice per day, for example, you may be offered your brand of medication in 250 mg tablets to be taken three times a day (which would give you 50 mg, or 6.3 percent, less per day than you're used to). If the numbers start to get confusing or don't sound right, ask the attending pharmacist or doctor to help you. Discuss if any slight difference in dosage is going to affect the treatment of your disorder.

Another problem is that your drug might not come in the pills you're used to, but in capsules that are very difficult to split. Ask the pharmacist for suggestions if you're used to cutting dosages in half. For additional information on filling a prescription abroad, visit the U.S. Embassy's website at
http://travel.state.gov/travel/tips/brochures/brochures_1215.html
before your trip.

Recognizing and Avoiding Counterfeit Medications

Counterfeit drugs are a worldwide problem contributing to illness, drug resistance, and even death. A counterfeit medication is not produced by an authorized manufacturer, but dispensed as if it were; both the pill and its packaging are often virtually identical to the authentic drug. Regulatory agencies in developed countries protect us from counterfeit meds, but in developing countries, regulatory controls are much less effective – or even nonexistent. Your chance of being offered counterfeit drugs for sale in a developing country can range from between fifteen and thirty percent.

If you're in a position of having to obtain medications locally, the last thing you'll want to worry about is whether they are "the real thing" or not. Since counterfeit drugs are not made by a legitimate manufacturer, they may contain hazardous contaminants that can cause you serious harm. The active ingredient may be present in small quantities, or substituted entirely by a cheaper compound that's less effective. In addition, the wrong inactive ingredients can contribute to poor drug distribution in your body, or lead to an adverse or allergic reaction.

Fortunately, there are ways to tell whether a local pharmacy is offering you a counterfeit.

Evaluate the physical properties. Be familiar with the precise size, shape, and color of your medication. Discoloration, spots, cracks, and stickiness of the capsules or tablets are indications of a possible counterfeit. Before you run out of medication, keep one last pill so you can compare it to what you are offered at a local pharmacy.

Taste. Although it's quite unappealing to familiarize with the taste of something that you typically swallow whole, knowing what your medication tastes like is a very effective way to discern real from counterfeit. Counterfeiters focus on the physical appearance of a drug

to fool you, and make additional "pharmaceutical" decisions based on how well the fake compound stands up to heat and moisture. Such compounds may taste drastically different from the genuine medication.

Original packaging. Be familiar with the packaging of your medication, and make sure that what you're being offered is in its original dispensing container. Different color inks, poor-quality print and misspellings, and different types of packaging material are all clues to counterfeit drugs. If you receive loose capsules or tablets in an envelope or a plastic bag, request to see where they came from.

Additional inquiries. If you're very suspicious about the prescription filled for you, request and record the batch number that the medication came from. Note the expiration date; if there's none listed, ask the pharmacist why, and look for other items that may be missing such as the side effects warning label. If you make a fuss, the pharmacist or assistant may take back what they've offered and tell you to come back in a while – at which time you may be offered the real thing, or suddenly told to go somewhere else. Do yourself a favor, and take them up on it.

Traveling with Other Emotional Health Problems

This book has focused on how to travel successfully with any of the four most common anxiety disorders. Besides PTSD, panic disorder, social anxiety disorder, or generalized anxiety disorder, many people suffer from an additional anxiety disorder such as obsessive-compulsive disorder or seasonal affective disorder. Other people may be diagnosed with one of the two most common mood disorders, depression and manic depression. This chapter goes over how to manage these other conditions in order to have an enjoyable and successful trip.

Obsessive-Compulsive Disorder (OCD)

OCD is characterized by intrusive thoughts and repetitive behaviors performed to reduce anxiety over doing or thinking about certain things. Some sufferers perform compulsive rituals because they inexplicably feel they have to; others act compulsively to mitigate the anxiety caused by particular thoughts. Typical OCD manifestations that affect travel include:

- Repeatedly checking that hotel doors are locked, and that you have all your belongings;

- Excessive sanitizing, washing, and worrying about germs;

- Incessant fear of handling currency, doorknobs, railings, and elevator buttons;

- Making sure certain items (whether they're your own or not) are arranged a certain way; and

- Counting buildings, people, shops, cars, trains, planes, and on and on.

On top of the uneasiness and fear that typically come with OCD (particularly if your manifestations are noticed by others), the amount of time spent performing compulsions every day can quickly drain the energy and joy out of your trip. Under the weight of trying to "sort" the new places, things, and people around you, your ability to stay mentally and emotionally healthy, and enjoy an ambitious sightseeing itinerary, may be under significant strain. Fortunately, there are a number of fairly straightforward ways to manage and prevent significant flare-ups, with a focus on minimizing time spent in certain places. Consider the following.

Casinos. Gambling meccas like Las Vegas and Macau are supposed to be some of the most fun places in the world to visit, but their hyperstimulating atmosphere, relentless automation, and fixations on quantities (money or odds) can severely aggravate even moderate OCD impulses. Unless the thrills outweigh the agitations, you might want to avoid them.

Megamalls. Like casinos, these are highly synthetic environments that are visually overwhelming and overly systematic; the level of detail alone can leave your mind reeling. If you want to shop, outdoor markets and small banks of souvenir shops are less likely to exacerbate your worst OCD tendencies.

Sites featuring supernatural or religious phenomena. Going to a place that celebrates or encourages rituals or recitations to keep negative forces away won't do your state of mind any favors. Get a book about the site instead, or visit a more traditional place of worship.

Sleeper trains. These can be nerve-wracking since you're trying to fall asleep amidst a number of intermittent and routine noises caused by traveling at normal to high speeds, while restless passengers cough, pace, or go through their own bedtime rituals nearby.

The metro. Having to board and disembark the correct train at the correct place within nine (or eight, or ten) seconds, with all your things, is going to wreak havoc on your OCD and your nerves. If you can't afford a taxi, opt for a bus since being part of a smaller, more personalized group of travelers will be less stressful – and there won't be as many pickpockets, so you won't be constantly checking for your items.

Here are some more preferable destinations and activities for OCD sufferers.

Beaches. These minimalist environments are effective at pulling you out of your head and back in touch with all five senses.

Cruises. You get to stay in the same place and keep the same stateroom (minimizing the perceived need to check for lost items) yet you're less likely to fall into a mental rut because the scenery is always changing. You may also find that being surrounded by so much water eases the rigid tendencies that OCD feeds on.

Concerts and symphonies. Hearing a piece of music for the first time, or listening to one you're familiar with played differently, can break all the "rules" in your head and be very enjoyable. Classical music is particularly effective since it tends to be less repetitive.

Camping. OCD sufferers tend to do better in natural environments. The predictable but simple cycle of day and night, coupled with the more unpredictable forces of weather and the living things around you, can disrupt and distract from many compulsive habits and thoughts.

Here are some general strategies to minimize the impact of OCD on your trip.

Recognize that you have a finite amount of energy. One of the most painful aspects of OCD is that it knows no limits; it can grow with a life of its own depending on what you're preoccupied with, and how much stress you're under. Traveling takes a lot of energy, and mistakes can compound faster than you can count the number of cobblestones down a sidewalk. If you check your bag several times to make sure you still have your camera, for example, you could miss your bus going by, with a string of potential consequences from there.

If you can't manage or distract yourself from your obsessions and compulsions, then try to "shift" them to something that's more relevant to your needs, such as counting the number of buses that go by.

Get enough sleep. When you are tired you're more likely to make mistakes and be forgetful, which can send your OCD into overdrive since you might actually leave something behind, or neglect to do something.

Know how to pace your trip. Spending too little time in one place can disrupt your sense of control and make you feel unorganized and overwhelmed; however, staying in the same place for too long can cause you to fall into a compulsive routine. The same characteristics that make you feel at home at a place (knowing every route in and out of a hotel, or where the best table in the breakfast room is) can also make you feel trapped within its system, and destroy the spontaneity of travel.

Three or four nights in one place might make you the most comfortable. If you're unsure at first, try double-booking hotels in different cities (and cancel one the day before the reservation) and arrange flexible transportation.

Hands off. There are two compulsions that tend to exacerbate one another: obsessive handling of certain items, and hand-washing or use of sanitizer. Stop touching things, and you'll feel less compelled to use sanitizer since you're not picking up the same number of germs. Keeping both hands occupied (e.g., carrying a bottle of water in one hand and a rolled-up newspaper in the other) can help you stay "hands off."

Use a compartmentalized bag or purse. If you have a specific place for everything in your bag, then taking a quick check (and not ten, accompanied by a considerable amount of rummaging) can ensure that everything is in its place. Travel with a gunny sack and you'll make yourself miserable (not to mention give yourself a couple of scares if you distractedly slip your wallet into your pocket instead of your bag).

LODGING PREFERENCES FOR OCD SUFFERERS

Independent hotels. Big-name and chain hotels tend to be formulaic, with the same design not only from hotel to hotel, but within the hotel itself. Seeing identical patterns and tiling over and over again in the lobby, on each floor, down each hallway, and in your room creates the systematic and repetitive environment that significantly aggravates OCD. Independent hotels tend to be more laid-back, quirky places, with inconsistent furnishings and harmless abnormalities that defy "categorization." You might find such a hotel far more relaxing.

One of the reasons chain hotels are popular is because people know what to expect of them, while locally-owned hotels can be hit-or-miss. The internet has changed that, with sites such as www.tripadvisor.com and www.hotels.com listing traveler reviews of even the smallest independent or family-owned lodgings. Reading these reviews can help you find a quality independent hotel.

Choose a smaller room. A smaller room means fewer places to put things, which means you won't spread out as much, and are less likely to leave something behind (or worry about leaving something behind).

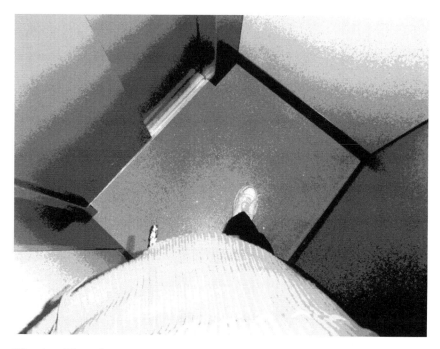

Bipolar Disorder

Bipolar disorder (also known as manic depression) is characterized by disruptive mood swings, and features elevated states known as mania alternated with bouts of depression. A distinct subset of anxiety sufferers also suffer from bipolar disorder – with the latter usually diagnosed first, and the anxiety disorder developing from the trauma of living as a manic depressive. Suffering from both disorders will present some unique, but not insurmountable, challenges to traveling. Here are some recommendations for ensuring a more enjoyable trip abroad.

Start with shorter trips. People with bipolar disorder commonly experience a manic episode for no longer than a week. Depending on how successful your current treatment is, and your overall excitement about and attitude towards your vacation, it's quite likely that you'll experience a manic episode shortly before or at the beginning of your trip. A week might be a wise duration of stay, at a closer destination, until you determine how to pace yourself during travel.

Another option is to build a lull into the middle of your trip to accommodate any depressive episode, followed by another week during which you "bounce back." Only you and your doctor know how long it takes to "bounce back," and you should put considerable thought into how you may feel at the beginning, middle, and end of your vacation before booking.

Physical activities that support moderation. Choose outdoor adventures that require consistency instead of impulse or calculation. This could include hiking or biking instead of bungee-jumping or rock climbing. Understand and respect that your ability and judgment may be adversely affected in an unfamiliar environment – and that there's nothing more hazardous than attempting risky feats in both a manic and anxious state.

Managing rage. In a manic state, you may experience severe irritability which can be compounded by anxiety over things turning out – or about to turn out – differently than you'd hoped. If there's a travel setback, you could have a hard time holding back your feelings, and encounter intolerance or reproach depending on how the local culture accepts displays of emotion. Some cultures (particularly Latin American, Southern European, and African) might be more tolerant than others (particularly Asian) so you should keep this in mind if you have a problem controlling your temper.

Flexible tours. Some tours are very structured, with a summons in the morning, afternoon, and evening that can sometimes feel like a cattle-call; others offer more independence, allowing you to select from several excursions per day, or to simply sit them out. A flexible tour will help you avoid frustration from being stuffed into a schedule that doesn't consider how you're feeling.

Seasonal Affective Disorder (SAD)

Seasonal affective disorder (SAD), also known as seasonal depression, is a mood disorder in which people experience significant depressive symptoms due to lack of sunlight. Symptoms of SAD can include difficulty waking up in the morning, difficulty completing tasks, a sense of hopelessness, and lack of energy. Although many tourists are inclined to choose "sun and sand" type destinations for a vacation, there are many beautiful and immensely popular places around the world that aren't exactly known for their uplifting climate. This section will help you prevent SAD from interfering with your enjoyment of those destinations.

For the sake of classifying SAD environments, tourist destinations can be characterized as one of the following:

➤ ***Usually overcast (cloudy or foggy).*** This includes popular cities such as London, Dublin, Copenhagen, Seattle, and Vancouver, as well as their surrounding regions of Northern Europe and the Pacific Northwest. They usually have a significant impact on SAD sufferers since they exhibit qualities of winter climates nine or more months per year.

➤ ***Constantly changing.*** Cities such as Auckland, Budapest, Tokyo, and Munich, and regions including Southeast Europe and the Canadian Atlantic fall into this category. The weather changes so frequently that you can feel like you're experiencing three or four seasons in one day. Some people might view this as getting

238

the best of everything at once; others might view it as a constant distraction and too tumultuous to deal with, particularly in the spring and summer when the cycle is usually more pronounced. These climates can have a moderate impact on SAD sufferers.

- ➤ *Usually sunny.* This includes Athens, Rome, and Madrid, and regions such as the Caribbean, the Middle East, and Southeast Asia. These climates can significantly impact sufferers of Reverse SAD. RSAD, or summer depression, affects a smaller subset of people than SAD and usually has the opposite symptoms, during summer months. The effects and management of RSAD are discussed further below.

Don't reconsider visiting a certain place just because it falls into a category that will aggravate your Seasonal Affective Disorder. Take a look at these recommendations instead.

Choose the right room. Ask for a room on one of the top floors of your place of lodging, and with a southern exposure (or a northern exposure if you are vacationing in the Southern Hemisphere).

Divide activities into indoor and outdoor. Build enough flexibility into your itinerary so that you can plan to be at a museum or shopping mall when the weather gets you down, and outside when the sun finally comes out.

Consider time of year. It may seem obvious, but avoid going on your trip during the six months or so when the weather is at its worst. A lot of people are tempted to travel off-season to save money, but you should consider the weather's role in exactly why places become unpopular at certain times of year. If London in January is going to make you miserable, then is saving $600 on airfare and hotels really going to make a difference to you? Can you reach a compromise by going in late spring to avoid both the constant fog and the summer crowds?

Go out at night. It will hardly matter if it's cloudy, or not. The bright lights of the city can be uplifting, and you may be wide awake anyway if you're jetlagged.

Take a portable light-box. Light therapy involves exposing yourself to a special incandescent lamp (light-box) which simulates the sun. Many lights are now travel-size and portable; your bigger challenge may be to keep on a light therapy schedule when traveling.

Take melatonin supplements. Melatonin can help you fall and stay asleep when you want in order to take advantage of the most daylight hours at your destination. These supplements are available over the counter at drugstores and at many big-box stores.

REVERSE SAD

It might be hard to imagine that some individuals recoil against what most perceive to be cheerful, sunny skies – but people with reverse SAD (or RSAD) long for the reflective, safe, and soothing feeling they get under a sky blanketed with clouds. RSAD sufferers often describe the sun as a large, overwhelming spotlight in a depressingly empty sky, with no place for them to escape or relax. RSAD manifestations include restlessness, insomnia, irritability, and constantly feeling overstimulated. If you suffer from this, then trying to enjoy regions such as Southern Europe, the Caribbean, India, and Southeast Asia can present a serious challenge. Here are some guidelines for managing RSAD.

Schedule outdoor activities for dawn or dusk. At these times, the dim sky can give the illusion of being overcast.

Pick the right accommodation. Reserve a room that faces a courtyard, is situated in a basement, or has no window at all. Not only will you avoid sunlight, but you're likely to save a lot of money.

If no such room is available, ask the receptionist for black-out curtains. Most hotels have at least a couple sets for those guests who stay out all night and come back to sleep at six in the morning.

Keep yourself as cool as possible since heat, sweating, and dehydration can all exacerbate your intolerance for sunlight.

Go when the days are short. Except at or near the equator, where day and night are roughly equal length year round, there are better times and worse times for RSAD sufferers to tour sunny climates. Scheduling your trip over winter solstice is ideal if you don't mind missing the holidays at home.

For more information on how climate impacts anxiety, refer back to Chapter 3.

Generalized Depression

Depression is a state of low mood and aversion to activity that can have a negative effect on your thoughts, behavior, world view, and physical well-being. You can feel hopeless, empty, sluggish, hurt, and irritable for inexplicable reasons, even when you have the opportunity to vacation and relax. If you suffer from depression on top of anxiety, you've jumped a major hurdle just by reading this book and deciding that it's worthwhile to take a trip. Your biggest challenge may be to stay interested and committed to your trip once you've arrived at your destination. Here are some travel strategies for managing depression.

Pick a bare-bones hotel. There are plenty of safe, simple, and uplifting hotels that offer a good night's sleep, a clean bathroom, and not a whole lot more. If you don't have a fancy room or a suite, you're less likely to barricade yourself in your hotel, and more likely to go outside and explore.

Most basic hotels lack both a bar and a restaurant, so if your depression runs hand in hand with a tendency to drink, there's one less temptation you have to worry about downstairs.

Have a plan, or ask for one. Since depression affects your ability to make decisions, you should think about what you'd like to do well before you arrive (and preferably at the time that you're most excited about the trip). If you show up in a city with no idea of what to do, ask the hotel receptionist for some suggestions. Even basic hotels will have receptionists who are eager to tell you where the great spots are – it's their home, after all, and they're usually proud of it.

Stay healthy. It's well-known that people with depression have lower levels of immunity since the mind and body are interdependent. Since you have a higher chance of getting sick abroad than at home, it's critical to take care of yourself. If you forgot (or didn't bother) to bring vitamins, go out and buy some, and if you're not drinking enough water because you're worried about tap water safety, purchase some bottled water as well. Take advantage of a local fitness center (budget hotels without their own centers often have contracts with nearby health clubs), and look for tourist attractions that promote health and wellness. Geothermal spas and bath houses are some such examples that are more prevalent overseas than you would think.

Schedule something great towards the end of your trip. You might be tempted to front-load your vacation with the things you most want to see because you know you'll have the most energy at the get-go. However, with nothing to look forward to after the first several days, you may lose energy, fall into a slump, and wish you were going home early. Search for something fun (and preferably cheap, since you'll most likely be running low on money) such as a local parade or May Day celebration for the last day or two of your vacation.

Share. If you make your vacation just about you, and you had a rough or uninspiring day, you may suffer from thoughts of worthlessness and question the value of continuing. You may not realize that your role as a visitor matters as much to others as it does to you – and not just for economic reasons. Answer (or invite) questions from a curious receptionist or shop clerk about how your destination compares to where you're from. You'll see your inherent value to people as you shed some color on a place that may have only existed in their imagination.

243

Go shopping. Fundamentally, shopping involves discovering new things, and different ways of doing things. Aside from the evils posted to its excesses, it can also be a relaxing way to learn about another culture. If you're worried about overspending, just take some cash and leave your credit cards in your room.

Get out and about. Many depressed people understand the difference between being *around* people, and being *with* people. Forcing yourself to be with people may cause you to recoil from social encounters and basic interactions, particularly since you also suffer from anxiety; being around people helps you keep your perspective and boosts your energy level.

Promise a treasure hunt for friends and family. Several of the people you like or love may hope you bring back souvenirs for them. Don't disappoint them; make a project out of searching for something they will find interesting. It doesn't have to come from a store; you can find natural keepsakes on a beach such as shells, rocks, or feathers.

Walk. Try to walk as much as you can – preferably outside. Not only will you decrease insomnia by getting more exercise; you'll also combat the lethargy, muscle tension, and psychosomatic aches and pains that often come with depression.

How Modern Technology Enables the Anxious Traveler

The internet, email, and software applications readily available on hand-held and tablet devices have all changed the landscape of traveling. They help you bring your plans to life, move around without getting lost, and stay in touch without having to figure out foreign payphones or deal with expensive hotel surcharges. Even if you've never been fully on board with the digital age, it's hard to deny that travel is less stressful when you have a screen and a keypad lying next to your passport.

Booking, Canceling, and Complaining: Making Use of the Internet and Email to Ease Anxiety

As someone who suffers from anxiety, the chances are you've developed good writing skills over the years because it's often the least stressful form of communication. Fortunately, modern technology has swayed in the favor of people who can present themselves clearly and concisely via email. You can now plan, book, salvage, adjust, and rebook a trip from start to finish without talking to a single human being. This isn't to say that you *have* to do all these things electronically, but those interactions that you used to flub because you were too nervous to present yourself well can now be handled a lot less stressfully.

Email also has the advantage of officiating arrangements that in the past were made only over the phone (and unfortunately, were often subject to change, or to luck in finding the same person who was helping you earlier). Even cultures that highly value face-to-face communication, and are prone to "informal agreements" (i.e., underhand favors for friends) find it hard to deny a reservation or arrangement (such as a room on the quieter side of the hotel, or early check-out) that has a trail of email attached to it. Here are some other advantages of using the internet and email.

No more relying on travel agents. One of the things that may have prevented you from traveling in the past was having to meet with, or phone, a travel agent. You may have dreaded relying on someone else's recommendations, and dealing with their constant persuasions, when you tried to explain the aspects of a trip that caused you the most stress and anxiety. Fortunately, travel agents aren't the gatekeepers they once were; you can still use one, but there are many other options. Sites including www.travelocity.com, www.orbitz.com, and www.expedia.com help you build and book a trip from start to finish, or purchase a package including flight, hotel, and secondary transportation (i.e. car rental).

You can cancel online as well, without the stress of someone trying to change your mind (and no one to feel bad about disappointing).

Bargaining. Some large discount travel retailers like Priceline.com have "name your own price" features that allow you to wheel and deal online for a plane or hotel ticket. If the website doesn't like your offer, "it" rejects or raises it, so any awkwardness is really between you and your computer, and you can simply try again for a bargain. You probably wouldn't work up the nerve to negotiate a lower price with a live travel agent, or even know when doing so may be appropriate.

Complaining. If you have trouble confronting people about deficient service and other problems (and most anxiety sufferers do), email makes it a lot easier to get something addressed without getting flustered, angry, or overwhelmed. For example, if a hotel receptionist is giving you the run-around and there's no one else onsite to take a look at your broken shower faucet, you don't have to demand to speak to their supervisor; you can go upstairs and look up the manager's email address online, and email your grievance. Whether they're in the back room or a hundred miles away, it's just as easy for the manager to email and instruct the receptionist to get you the service you need.

Utilizing Augmented Reality Mobile Applications to Locate Pharmacies, Medical Clinics, and Just About Anything Else

We've talked a lot about being able to find a pharmacy, hospital, or medical clinic in a foreign city. Even if you get good directions from your psychiatrist or from the U.S. Embassy (and particularly if one of your biggest travel fears is getting lost) you may want to take advantage of an application called augmented reality, or AR, to help you navigate abroad. AR is a live view of your real-world environment, captured on a screen and narrated by computer-generated input (usually text, but also graphics, sound and GPS data). Imagine standing in a foreign street and holding a smart phone out, like a camera, and having the names and uses of each building in front of you pop up on the screen. This can be invaluable for identifying one of the many thousands of pharmacies across the world *not* marked with a cross symbol – or one of the many more hospitals or clinics that look like something else entirely.

AR hardware usually consists of a processor, a display, and sensors (all three of which are rolled into one unit and shaped to fit your hand) and the output device (usually a headset, which may not be necessary depending on how easy your display is to use). Standalone units were common at first, but more and more, smart phones and tablets have the camera, sensor, and output needed to support AR. In mid-2013, the application (including all the required software) cost between $400 and $600. If you want to explore on your own but are anxious about your poor sense of direction or inability to navigate, AR can make a great, worthwhile tool. Here are some things it can particularly help you with:

- Identifying the full route of a bus you see down the street;
- Opening and closing hours of a museum or shopping center;
- Potential hazards in your path (such as poorly marked construction);
- Road conditions and traffic updates (if you are driving); and last

but not least,
- Translating foreign text on signs and menus.

Some drawbacks of using AR include:
- Dangerous levels of immersion. Don't get so absorbed in the interface that you become oblivious to your surroundings. AR will tell you a lot, but not about the bad habits of drivers or the motivations of the people around you.
- Just as with a Professional Travel Companion, you can become dependent on AR. Consider the possible effect on your confidence, and your ability to develop into a self-reliant traveler.
- The application can take some of the discovery and personal experience out of your trip. If part of your touring enjoyment comes from figuring out where a particular park path leads, or whether an odd building is a museum or an antiques store, then save AR for more serious and practical matters.

Communicating with Your Doctor While Abroad

Most supportive psychiatrists will agree to maintain contact with you while you're traveling. There are several good reasons for keeping in touch, including 1) continuity of care; 2) assistance your doctor may be able to provide in locating a pharmacy or care abroad; and 3) your peace of mind. You should talk to your psychiatrist at least a couple weeks before your trip about how you will communicate. Here are some things to consider.

Phone vs. email communication. To avoid time zone differences, and the obvious expense, you might prefer to email rather than phone your psychiatrist while abroad. Keep in mind, though, that your doctor is used to being able to observe your body language and identify other physical cues when treating you, and might request phone consultation so that he or she can at least clue in to the sound of your voice (and sense any hesitation, fear, doubts, etc.) before making any determinations. A lot of it depends on how well your doctor knows you, and how well you're able to communicate your symptoms in writing.

Suitable activities. A doctor is rarely, if ever, going to give you outright approval (or disapproval) to do certain things; ultimately, you're the one who decides what you do. What your doctor *can* do is provide guidance and reassurance, and weigh the pros and cons of different activities with you based on the information you share about what you want to try.

Past treated issues. If an old anxiety trigger flares up while you're traveling, your doctor can help you decide whether avoidance or controlled confrontation will be best.

Currently treated issues. Your doctor is very unlikely to be able to diagnose a new problem or disorder without seeing you, but should be able to respond regarding new symptoms you experience that relate to an existing diagnosis.

Uncomfortable topics. If there was a question you didn't ask before you left because you were just plain embarrassed (such as how to deal with a certain phobia), the logic "it's better late than never" applies.

Finding local care. When asking your psychiatrist for assistance in finding a local pharmacy or psychiatric care, ask him or her for a landmark and cross-street in addition to the street address. This is usually easy for your doctor to do using modern mapping technologies, and can save you a lot of effort second-guessing places at your destination.

Help identifying counterfeit drugs. If you've had a bad experience at a nearby pharmacy, and couldn't reach your psychiatrist by phone when filling the prescription, send him or her a photo of the medications you just bought and ask for assistance in identifying a counterfeit. You'll already have spent the money with no way of returning the item, but you may spare yourself taking something that's dangerous.

Health insurance questions. If you need to choose between certain types of care and coverage, your doctor may be sympathetic to the challenge of navigating an HMO bureaucracy from abroad, and triage questions for you.

The Journey Back from the Other Side of the Horizon

Bringing your vacation to a close can be a rewarding and emotional experience. You may feel euphoric, proud, reborn, grateful, fulfilled, and like a different person. After you've seen, done, and been a part of many incredible things abroad, it can be hard to move on – and even more challenging to remember exactly how you viewed the world, and your life, before your trip. In the following pages we'll look at how to put things into perspective, and anticipate how and why you may feel different upon returning home. You'll learn about what post-trip symptoms you need to share with your psychiatrist, and how to bring closure to your trip by talking to your travel companion. We'll look at how your trip may inspire a number of changes to your everyday life – and how to make them without overwhelming yourself. Finally, you'll take a deeper look at what you've accomplished as a traveler and a person, and how to connect with other anxiety sufferers as you continue to take incredible trips in the future.

Moving On: How to Leave a Place without Stress

According to Buddhism, the root of all suffering is attachment – wisdom you may certainly understand when it's time to leave your travel destination. Considering that a certain beach, café, park, hotel, or other favorite locale existed only in your imagination weeks before, your connection to a place and reluctance to leave can be intense. Managing these feelings is important since you don't want them to overcome the joy of having seen them in the first place – or as the pessimistic traveler laments, *Why come if I only have to leave?*

Besides understanding that you can't see or appreciate the next incredible place if you never move on, you should acknowledge some of the larger questions plaguing your subconscious, such as:

- Will I ever come here again?

- What will happen here after I leave?

- How will this place change without me? Can it be "mine?"

- Does it matter that I ever came here?

These feelings and doubts can resemble separation anxiety. How significant this anxiety is depends on 1) how much of an emotional connection you've made to a place, and 2) how difficult it is to physically make your way back to it. The answers to those two questions can vary widely, but here are some general recommendations for moving on without trauma.

Take a piece with you. There's a reason that the souvenir industry is valued at billions of dollars; people want a symbol or a token of their experience somewhere, even if their only "connection" with it was at a local club. If you don't care for either synthetic, mass-produced trinkets or museum-type expensive souvenirs, then take a piece of a place, literally: some stones, shells, a feather, or a piece of wood or bark. Holding these items long after you've left can put you back in the moment of your tremendous experience.

Leave a piece of yourself. More tourists than would care to admit leave a part of themselves behind at a place they love – anything from a strand of hair to engravings on a tree, to things that border on defacement or ecological damage. An environmentally friendly way to leave your mark is to pen your name and the date on a small, loose rock and put it back where it was on a trail or thoroughfare.

Metaphysically inspired travelers may try relinquishing an anxiety trigger or phobia at a place they love, but won't be back to.

Keep a travel log. A travel log doesn't have to take the form of a written journal; depending on how much you (don't) like to write, you can tape- or video-record your experiences and impressions. Another option is to keep a notebook, but only record the facts, events, and people you encountered each day. Your memory will fill in the rest of the details as you mentally journey back later on.

You can also draw on a map where you went, with brief notes at each street or block that will remind you of something special; or pick a new piece of music to play while you are enjoying the place, that will always remind you of where you were when you first heard it.

Virtual visits. If your time at a place is too limited for you to manage a travel log, note that there are thousands of YouTube internet videos featuring beloved travel sites, and they are viewable by anyone. Some of them are amazingly done and might even showcase something you never noticed about a place. Although it's not going to be as special or personalized as something you put together, knowing you can make a "virtual visit" can help you move on.

Plan to return. Promise yourself to come back to the place. If you've come once, you can come again, and most incredible sites don't just get up and leave. They can evolve, however, so keep abreast of the place by going to its webpage. If you find out that it's destined to change (and not necessarily to your liking), time an upcoming visit to enjoy it one more time as you remembered it.

Seeing Your Doctor after Your Trip

Even if you had a generally enjoyable and successful vacation, you should plan to see your psychiatrist within a month of returning home for a post-travel evaluation. This should include talking about experiences that were painful or difficult, as well as those that might have been overwhelming and left you with unresolved feelings. Other items to discuss during the follow-up visit include:

- Any travel activities that resulted in loss of confidence;

- Phobias you may have exacerbated or developed;

- Any correspondence the two of you exchanged during your trip, as well as any that your psychiatrist received directly from an attending physician at your destination; and

- Any panic or anxiety attacks that you had, and what you could do in the future to better manage or prevent them.

There are some instances when you should plan to see your psychiatrist as soon as possible to address problems or feelings that started right after, or even towards the end of, your trip. These include:

Intense flashbacks of near-misses or traumas during your trip, such as almost being hit by a bicyclist; mistreatment or abuse of power by police; or loss or theft of baggage. These flashbacks may be accompanied by delusions of actual events (where you're unable to distinguish a memory from images of what could have happened).

Being unable to unpack or move on from the trip because you have so many raw emotions, or feel debilitated with reluctance and uncertainty. This can be coupled with an inability to remember entire days of your trip, or an intense feeling that you haven't gone anywhere at all and that your trip is still to come.

Physical disturbances such as dizziness, disrupted sleep, and exhaustion that don't go away with recovery from acute travel fatigue or jet lag. You should also discuss any psychosomatic symptoms such as muscle aches or pains that aren't a result of soreness from activity during your trip.

Significant disorientation where your own environment and way of doing things seem bizarre and unfamiliar. This can include being unable to remember how you functioned before your vacation, and impatience or frustration at work, with friends, and with family. Other symptoms include repeatedly waking up in your own bed and being unsure of where you are, and wondering how or why your loved ones recognize you.

All of these manifestations can occur in anxiety sufferers who took on too much, too fast. Even if your chaotic trip was enjoyable, your mind and body are treating it like a trauma of sorts that requires a recovery period. When addressing these particular problems, try to acknowledge with your doctor that you overdid it – otherwise you could take out your distress and frustration on any future trips you want to take, rather than acknowledging that how fast and how hard you toured is responsible for how you feel.

The good news is that these disturbances usually don't last, as long as you confront them early by discussing them with your psychiatrist.

Finally, if you suffered a number of physiological disruptions during your trip that were clearly due to medication side effects, you might be wondering if there's a different medication out there that's a better neurochemical fit for you, and will treat your anxiety symptoms just as well. There's nothing wrong with questioning your meds, particularly if your significant side effects are something you've been putting up with in your daily life for quite some time. Traveling and the enjoyment it brings often inspires people to expect (or at least hope for) a higher quality of life, and that can include wanting all the benefits of a drug without all of the drawbacks.

It takes a lot of courage to consider going off a certain medication to try something new, especially if (despite its drawbacks) your existing medication helped enable you to travel. Share all of your thoughts and feelings with your psychiatrist, and be sure not to suddenly stop taking your pills or modify your dose until you've come to a decision with him or her.

Talking to Your Travel Companion After Your Trip

Besides talking to your doctor about the psychological impacts of your trip, it's essential to discuss the highlights and lowlights of your journey with any relative(s) or friend(s) who traveled with you. Your anxiety disorder shouldn't be the focal topic, but one of several as you discuss your experiences together, and compare yourself to how they are adjusting to being back home.

If you think such a conversation will be awkward and too emotionally loaded, waiting another week or two can make a big difference since you'll both be better rested and have a better perspective, but your memories are still fresh. Don't feel pressured to talk about taking future trips together; there will be plenty of time for that.

If you toured with a Professional Travel Companion, recognize that they'll usually be happy to discuss your trip with you, and the conversation won't be as personal or intense as with a relative or friend. This may also be the time that you have to part with your PTC, since 1) you may not need him or her for future vacations, or 2) even if you want him or her to join you on another trip, it may not be a location that they serve, and they can't be your companion. If this is the case, consider your PTC a friend to email future trip photos or stories to, and move on.

Here are some specific things to go over with your travel companion.

When they worried about you. There may have been stressful times during your trip when you felt you were in control, but it appeared otherwise to your companion, and they were very concerned about your well-being. Discussing these scenarios with the person can reassure them and can also clue you in to personal behaviors you may not be aware of, that could cause you to be misunderstood in the future.

What could have been better. Discuss what caused some irritation and frustration on both sides – such as where you depended on your companion too much, when they were too self-absorbed or dropped the ball, or when neither of you communicated well. This should be an exchange, not a blame-game; if it causes you stress, let your travel companion talk about these things first. One of the main goals is to think about future roles and responsibilities if you travel with this person again (i.e., who is better to do what) as well as some of your shortcomings as a traveler that could put you in a stressful situation if you're with someone else, or alone.

What really worked. Before things get too heavy, talk about things that turned out well either because of good planning, or good luck. Acknowledging when you were at your best, and feeling your best, will build your confidence, and as far as luck goes, there's often a lot that you can learn from it.

Close calls. There may be scenarios that you replay in your mind because they almost led to a major problem, such as nearly getting separated from your companion while boarding a flight, or being followed by someone until the two of you reached your hotel. You should talk about what led up to these events, the details you were missing, and what neither of you are still sure of. This takes the intimidation out of scary moments before they can develop into stressful flashbacks. You may even be able to make light of some of your close calls, or admit how obvious it was what you should have done at the time.

Understanding How Your Trip Can Impact Your Everyday Life

For something that lasted only about two or three weeks, a trip can have a tremendous influence on how you think, feel, and act for months and even years to come. You may want to make a number of changes to your everyday life that are very positive, but potentially overwhelming. Some of these changes are easy to make; others take far more energy and time to think about. Knowing *before* you leave on your trip that you may experience unusual feelings and impulses upon your return will help you avoid the stress of "culture shock" to your own life.   Here are some post-travel effects that are common among anxiety sufferers.

PHYSICAL EFFECTS

Becoming more active. When you travel, you might realize that you're not in the shape you thought you were, and as you gradually increase your fitness level during your trip, you may notice how much better you feel. This can inspire you to join a gym or take up a sport (including one you tried on your vacation) when you return. Becoming more active will not only make it easier to be in shape for the next trip; it can mitigate some of the regular side effects of your anxiety medication.

Restlessness. Traveling comes with a certain intensity and compression that can be difficult to unwind from. It also has the effect of "slowing" time, since you often do more different and eye-opening things in a single day than you might in a week at home. When you return, the restlessness you get from not doing something "new and different" every few hours is notably different than what you may experience as an anxiety sufferer, or as a side effect from medications. This restlessness usually goes away within six weeks of settling back into your everyday life. If you have the time, take smaller day trips in the weeks after your return to wear it off; otherwise, don't worry about it.

EMOTIONAL AND PSYCHOLOGICAL EFFECTS

"Travel rebound." If you had a great trip, you may not even recover from jet lag before you start thinking of booking the next vacation.

You may be afraid of these feelings because you fear they're compulsive, reactive, or will lead to a fixation on travel that you can't control.

Understand that many people start dreaming of their next vacation in order to minimize the "downer" that often comes with getting back to your job, chores, etc. Plenty of travelers liken "traveling on the rebound" to "dating on the rebound": as in, you miss the feeling of something so much that you can't wait to jump back in. Fortunately, booking travel on the rebound is a lot healthier, and more successful than dating on the rebound! If you're suffering from "travel rebound," don't be overly concerned as long as you're not extending yourself beyond your physical, financial, and practical means. It's when your credit card company starts calling, or (more importantly) your friends, family, and psychiatrist start to think of you as an escapist rather than a travel buff that you need to step back and look more at your home life than your passport.

Clear feelings. As anxiety sufferers, one of the things we have a hard time distinguishing is what we don't like, from what we're afraid of. As travel exposes you to more activities and you have a chance to overcome your fears of various things, people, or places, your personal preferences become clearer, and you understand yourself better. It's a great feeling to be able to state (to yourself or to others) that you dislike a particular activity, rather than knowing it has the power of dread over you.

Pondering dramatic changes. Taking your trip might make you realize that something is missing from your life, or that you've been *existing* rather than *living*. You may question where you've chosen to call home, what you do for a living, what activities you choose outside work, and even such things as your political or religious beliefs. This can be bewildering for the people who love you, but didn't accompany you on your trip; no matter how logical your feelings are to you, people may not understand your conviction to take a shrewd look at what's "always worked in the past."

As with most things in life, you usually end up with a compromise between your wishes, and what's practical. Wanting to suddenly quit your job or put your house up for sale may materialize into cutting your work hours while you try something you really want to do, or renting a lake house a two-hour drive away. You should be concerned about acting on your feelings without input from people you trust (especially if they will be impacted by your decisions). If you make a radical choice that you later regret, you may backlash against your vacation and against travel in general.

LIFESTYLE EFFECTS

Cleaning house. Living out of a suitcase can make you realize just how little you need to lead a full life. A lot of people are inspired to unload a number of items from their home after they return from vacation, and find it convenient to host a garage sale or sell items on eBay in order to make money for the next trip.

Having fewer possessions can also focus you more on your present life, and give you a far greater sense of freedom.

Starting hobbies. During a trip you're exposed to a myriad of new and different things – or the same things that you are used to, but in a different context. A common hobby you may take up after returning home is learning how to cook a certain ethnic food, or studying the language of a place you plan to revisit. As long as you keep it fun, these types of new activities will rarely cause you more anxiety.

Reassessed spending habits. Spending money on your traditional and more passive hobbies, such as on antique furniture or a DVD collection, might fall by the wayside as funding your next vacation shoots to the top of your priority list. This is generally healthy and fine as long as it's not taken to extremes, and you don't suddenly stop financing things that promote your mental and emotional health, such as music that helps you relax, or weekly meditation classes.

SOCIAL EFFECTS

Needing to share. To relive positive memories, you may be unable to resist telling others a lot about your trip – even if you've never shared much of anything with anyone. Since people are generally curious to hear firsthand experiences of other places and cultures, your chances of being rebuffed are pretty minimal. To coworkers and people who don't know you well, you become known as "the traveler," which makes a great icebreaker and can ease anxiety every time you see someone that you didn't feel comfortable talking to before.

Externalization. If you're very introverted, you may surprise yourself by engaging far more with coworkers, strangers, and acquaintances than usual when you return. This is a normal result of being constantly around people on a trip, and becoming desensitized to anxiety caused by casual interactions. In addition, you will often experience a period of feeling more laid-back, uninhibited, and spontaneous than normal.

Getting back into the groove of your everyday routine usually comes with a significant degree of reinternalization, so the feeling won't last forever. Of course, if you think your anxiety has been masking a lot of healthy extroversion you didn't know you had, then talk to your psychiatrist about it.

With all the possible effects your trip can have on how you think and live, it's obvious you need to give yourself time and energy to process your inspiration and your doubts. This means 1) not burning yourself out at the end of your trip, and 2) considering a day or two off in the weeks after your vacation. If you let yourself get overwhelmed, you could have a hard time distinguishing what is normal versus extreme post-vacation behavior – i.e., do something reckless or impulsive just so your thoughts will stop swirling. Always put a priority on recognizing thoughts or activities that affect your mental and emotional health.

Take a few minutes right now to think about how you will feel after your vacation.

What do you think will be the most challenging aspect of getting back to your everyday life?

_____

_____

What can you do before you leave to make this easier to manage?

_____

_____

How do you think your vacation may change you or how you view your life?

_____

_____

Do you think you'll have the time and energy after your trip to manage these feelings? If not, what can you do right now to ease your post-vacation schedule?

_____

_____

From Here to There

On the flight home from your destination, you should take some time to think about the magnitude and greatness of what you've done on your vacation, even if you had some rough days and stressful moments. As soon as you stepped on the ground of another country, you confronted your anxiety head-on. You didn't just seize the moment; you stayed *in* the moment. You started to balance your need for adventure with your need for psychological safety. You didn't give up. You were honest with yourself about what you could do, and when you needed to back off. You managed your fears and limitations while seeing and doing so many of the things the world has to offer.

Think about the six stages of classic Cognitive Behavioral Therapy we talked about in Chapter 2: assessment, reconceptualization, acquiring skills, developing adaptive coping strategies, generalization and maintenance, and post-treatment assessment follow-up. Your trip, and the weeks right after it, will have taken you through the whole process – meanwhile, if you weren't out having the time of your life, you were making yourself a stronger and more determined person, without ever thinking you were undergoing "therapy."

Besides not thinking about therapy, you might not have thought about the spiritual significance of your trip until now, or had a chance to give thanks – to God, or to others if you're not overly religious. Personally, I like to give thanks to the people I never met, who made my trip possible and enjoyable: the pilots who landed me safely, the conductors who steered my trains carefully, the airport staff who handled my bags gently even though they were probably tired and stressed out themselves – and the reservations staff over the phone and email who were just a little more patient and understanding than they're probably paid for, just so I could be smoothly on my way.

You might take a few minutes now to think about who and what you're grateful for, and write this down.

_____

_____

_____

Now, looking back on your trip, reflect on some of the most pivotal moments and experiences when your perceptions of yourself or the world forever changed. When you had to rise above your circumstances or your environment. When you were overcome with a before-and-after sense of having evolved as a human being... as well as times when you discovered something true about yourself and your journey. Try to complete the following.

What I was afraid to do on my trip, and did anyway:

_____

_____

What I was afraid to do, and will do next time:

_____

_____

Things I made too difficult:

_____

_____

What I never thought I'd pull off:

_____

What I finally saw for what it really is:

_____

_____

My "now what?" moments:

_____

_____

My best decisions:

_____

_____

What have you learned about your desire to travel?

_____

_____

_____

_____

_____

_____

Remember that exercise in the beginning of this book when you decided where you want to "go"? Now that you've taken your trip, decide where you've been, and where you are now. If you've gone from nervous to brave, give yourself due credit, and write it in; then decide where you want to "go" next (bold, adventurous, daring, etc.). Keep in mind that there's no timeline for getting from *here* to *there*, and no one to judge your personal journey.

I went from _____ **to** _____

and now I want to go from _____ **to**

_____ .

Over the years on board British Airways, Delta, Scandinavian Air, KLM, United, Iberia, All Nippon Airways, Air New Zealand, IcelandAir, and Air Canada flights, I've been able to engage with other anxiety sufferers reliving and summing up key moments of their vacation. I've found many of their remarks so inspiring that I've kept a small notebook of them, and I'll share with you some of their actual quotes.

"*What* anxiety?"

"You know, I've been existing instead of living."

"How many continents are there on the planet? Only seven?"

"No one in that entire bloody country gets stressed out over *any*thing."

"My fear was sure messing me up."

"God, what would a tourist think of my life?!"

"I said to the officer, '*You can have my money, just don't take my passport*'."

"What an eye-opener... now I see why I've driven myself nuts at home" *(joking)*.

"Well, there's nothing like expanding your horizons."

"And that $&#@ told me I wouldn't be able to survive two days outside the U S of A."

"I didn't know I could be such a _____ until I _____ with a _____." *(countless variations)*

"Self-gratification sure makes me feel better."

"I'm not the ideal traveler, but neither are those other folks!"

"I shoulda done this *years* ago."

"I deserve my own happiness, don't I?"

To share and connect more with other anxiety sufferers, go to www.theanxioustraveler.com, which is continually updated with resources and issues affecting travelers with anxiety disorders. You can exchange with me or others about a trip you're planning that includes bigger challenges, more countries, taller mountains, smaller islands, wider rivers, larger skyscrapers, and more cultural gems than you've ever contemplated before. Whatever you decide, you'll realize that with travel, the possibilities truly are endless – where you go, what you do, during what season, how and with whom, at what stage of your life, and why. The only really troubling question becomes, then:

What will you do with your armchair?

ABOUT THE AUTHOR

Rita Anya Nara has traveled through over forty countries on all seven continents despite being diagnosed with panic disorder, social anxiety disorder, and seasonal affective disorder. She earned a B.S. in Environmental Toxicology from the University of California at Davis in 2000 after completing specialized research on the effects of foreign environments and stimuli on brain chemistry and function. Her journey "from armchair to plane seat" has been profiled in *The Chicago Tribune, ABC Online, The AAA Show, Rudy Maxa's Travel Show, The Good Day Sacramento Show, Yahoo Finance, Fox Business, World Travelers of America, Travel Industry Today, VoiceAmerica, The Sacramento Bee, RadioMD,* and *WorldNews.com.* Nara resides in Northern California with two suitcases always packed at the foot of her bed.

Made in the USA
San Bernardino, CA
17 December 2013